WHY GOD?

WHY GOD?

Stories to Inspire Faith

Richard Leonard, SJ

Paulist Press
New York / Mahwah, NJ

Cover image by Hybrid_Graphics/Shutterstock.com
Cover and book design by Lynn Else

Library of Congress Cataloging-in-Publication Data
Names: Leonard, Richard, 1963– author.
Title: Why God? : stories to inspire faith / Richard Leonard, SJ.
Other titles: Tablet.
Description: New York ; Mahwah, NJ : Paulist Press, [2024] | Selection of 52 articles by the author written for The Tablet 2014–2024. | Summary: "This book brings together stories of faith that speak of the presence of God working in the lives of individuals and within the community. This book is a collection of articles written for The Tablet in the UK. Permission has been granted and they have been adapted slightly to reflect the current time and audience"—Provided by publisher.
Identifiers: LCCN 2023020455 (print) | LCCN 2023020456 (ebook) | ISBN 9780809156610 (paperback) | ISBN 9780809188222 (ebook)
Subjects: LCSH: Presence of God. | Faith (Christianity)—Catholic Church. | Catholic Church—Doctrines.
Classification: LCC BT180.P6 L46 2024 (print) | LCC BT180.P6 (ebook) | DDC 231.7—dc23/eng/20231031
LC record available at https://lccn.loc.gov/2023020455
LC ebook record available at https://lccn.loc.gov/2023020456

ISBN 978-0-8091-5661-0 (paperback)
ISBN 978-0-8091-8822-2 (e-book)

Published by Paulist Press
997 Macarthur Boulevard
Mahwah, New Jersey 07430
www.paulistpress.com

Printed and bound in the
United States of America

For my grandniece, Hazel; Margaret and David;
Marita and Bill; Jules, Lisa, Serena, Moira, and Zubin;
Ciara and Shane; Nena and Simon; Mark and Liz;
Colleen; Brian and Grant; Belinda and Trent;
Caroline and Bern; Josh, Duncan, and Maria;
Dorothy, Susan, and Anthony; Fay, Angela, Robyn,
and Ron; Maryann, Helen, Mary, Maureen,
John, and Mary; Denise and Chris; Marie and Jay;
Susan, Marie, Siobhan, and Patrick;
Patricia and Ray; Julie and Craig; Ignatius,
Jo, and Bob; Tony and Nancy; Sally and Louis;
and Mark and Cathy

CONTENTS

CONTENTS

Contents

FOREWORD

I remember a wonderful feature in *The Tablet* not too long ago when Morag MacInnes, a Scottish writer, remembered her friend, the brave, gentle Orkney poet George Mackay Brown. His work is permeated by his Catholicism. And he once asked, "How do I, as a poet and a writer, present holiness to a Godless generation? Especially as I know nothing about it myself?"

How do we put before the world holiness, forgiveness, reconciliation, prayer, when readers are no longer familiar with that kind of language? This is something every editor of *The Tablet*—every editor of a contemporary religious publication—has to wrestle with. And it's a rope trick that gets more difficult to pull off in every generation as the gap between the imaginative world of the person of faith and the humdrum vocabulary and horizon of the contemporary reader yawns ever wider. How do we find writers who are bilingual—who can speak the language of the world and the language of heaven?

When I was asked to take over from Catherine Pepinster as editor of *The Tablet* at Christmas 2016, I felt like the cat that got the cream. *The Tablet* was rooted in the traditions of the Church but delighted in the things of God it found in the modern world. It was 180 years old but didn't look it. It was interested in everything and everyone, particularly the things going on in the corner of the picture. It was intelligent, a tiny bit intimidating, but in a way that intrigued and invited engagement. The news reporting was crisp and even; the feature writing was gorgeous. It made some people nervous of course. It was in no one's pocket. It had its enemies. But it didn't belittle or sneer at them. And there was no bossy shepherding of people into heaven along tightly prescribed routes. *The Tablet* was a living, growing personality— faithful, honest, generous, inquisitive, irrepressibly reform-minded, and its readers loved it. I just hoped I wouldn't drop the Ming vase.

Although the job came with a rich inheritance of talent, a switch of captain inevitably leads to a change of bowling, the departure of a middle-order batter or two whose touch was beginning to desert them. But there were several names on Catherine's team sheet I greedily scooped up. And no one, Catherine and I agreed, was more fluently bilingual than Richard Leonard. I was quick to rope him into service under the new administration.

As you will see in this selection of some of his pieces for *The Tablet* over the years, Richard is a great noticer in the Ignatian tradition. He sees the grandeur behind the routine and the banal. He is wide-eyed and compassionate, infinitely curious and inquisitive. *Where the Hell Is God?*; *Why Bother Praying?*; *What Are We Doing On Earth for Christ's Sake?*; *What Does It All Mean?*; *What Are We Hoping For?*; *What Are We Waiting For?*; and now, *Why God?* Richard has a fondness for asking questions. He doesn't pretend to have all the answers, and he doesn't pretend the Church does either. The teaching of the Church is not a closed system; it does not tidy up every loose end or stifle every doubt. Its precepts are not electric fences to prevent us from straying into wickedness but springboards to propel us toward happiness and flourishing. The genius of Catholicism is precisely that it is not seeking to find rest in one register or settlement. It lives in the flashes of movement between them.

Smart, sometimes astringent, passionate; he can stroke and tease and puncture; there is tenderness and bite; reverence for life, joy, beauty, thankfulness; lightness, warmth, and good humor; the occasional sting—Richard's voice has helped me understand and shape *The Tablet*'s voice.

Richard Leonard is one of the canniest, sharpest, sweetest voices in the English-speaking Catholic world.

Brendan Walsh

ACKNOWLEDGMENTS

Mark-David Janus, CSP, Paul McMahon, Bob Byrns, and the team at Paulist Press for their continuing belief in my work, and for enabling me to talk to a very wide audience about faith and culture.

Vu Kim Quyen, SJ, and the Australian Province of the Society of Jesus for the education and formation I have received, and their ongoing support to do the "greatest good for the greatest number."

Brendan Walsh and his team at *The Tablet*; Catherine Pepinster, who initially invited me to write for that great journal; and our loyal readers for their encouragement.

The Jesuit community and parish of North Sydney, Australia, who give me many and various ways to encounter God.

INTRODUCTION

When I started studying theology in 1981, *The Tablet* was such an important weekly journal that, at great expense, it was airmailed from London to the seminary in Brisbane. It was essential reading for everyone. It was asserted at the time that it was read by "every English-speaking bishop in the world." It mattered. *The Tablet* wielded influence. Founded by the layman Frederick Lucas in 1840, only the *Spectator* is an older journal that is still in print in the United Kingdom.

Over the last 183 years, contributors have included Evelyn Waugh, Graham Greene, Pope Benedict XVI (as Cardinal Joseph Ratzinger), Pope Paul VI (as Cardinal Giovanni Battista Montini), Hans Küng, Eamon Duffy, Nicholas Lash, Rowan Williams, Gerald O'Collins, SJ, Tony Blair, Gordon Brown, and John Cornwell. Since 1935, *The Tablet* has been owned by laypeople, which gave it more freedom than many other Catholic journals owned and controlled by bishops, dioceses, or religious orders. This feature was evident in its reporting of the Second Vatican Council and its opposition to Pope Paul VI's encyclical *Humanae Vitae* on artificial contraception.

In 2004, Catherine Pepinster became the first

WHY GOD?

woman editor of *The Tablet*, stating at the time that "the journal will continue to provide a forum for progressive, but responsible Catholic thinking, a place where orthodoxy is at home, but ideas are welcome." In the wake of my book *Where the Hell Is God?*, Catherine asked me to write a feature article. In 2013, she commissioned an Advent series, and so began my regular contributions to a journal that I had long admired. In 2017, Brendan Walsh became the editor, and the relationship happily continued.

This volume is a selection of fifty-two articles published over the last ten years. It was the idea of my gifted and patient editor and good friend, Paul McMahon. He deserves any credit for this book. Paul sifted through all *The Tablet* articles over the years to reap the harvest from which, please God, you will soon benefit. Paul collected them into the major themes of Church, Liturgy and Sacraments, Society, and Faith and Discipleship. As a writer, it is always a fascinating journey to look back on one's work. There are, herein, issues, people, and events that I'd long let pass but that now have again rejoined my active consciousness. I am the richer for that. Some of these articles reveal a particular time, place, or circumstance. Though I hope the general point or principle is as applicable today as it was when I originally wrote them, there are only three occasions where I have updated the text because my own thinking needed to grow and mature in the light of other and better thoughts or ideas. We are all a work-in-progress.

I often quote my mother, Joan, because she is a font of good stories and the unvarnished truth. After I wrote a series of books with question marks in the title: *Where the Hell Is God?*; *Why Bother Praying?*; *What Are We Doing*

Introduction

On Earth for Christ's Sake?; *What Does It All Mean?*; *What Are We Hoping For?*; and *What Are We Waiting For?*, my mother said, "Can you please stop asking questions and give us the answers soon?" At the time of writing, she has advanced dementia, which sees her never stop asking questions. It might be the human condition stripped bare. I can only imagine her eyes rolling at the title, *Why God?* Depending on the emphasis one puts on the two words in the title, the reader is invited into a multilayered dialogue about faith and culture in an increasingly unbelieving society. I hope these reflections—one for every week of the year—give you some inspiration to keep asking questions about this world and the one to come.

PART ONE

CHURCH

1

A LISTENING CHURCH

A couple of weeks ago I was waiting at a train station when I was accosted by an earnest-looking young man. I must have looked like I needed some redeeming.

"Have you given your life to Jesus Christ as your personal Lord and Savior?"

"As a matter of fact, I have."

"Do you speak in tongues?"

"Well, as an unreconstructed Catholic charismatic, I can, but I choose not to because I don't find it a helpful form of communication."

"How do you know that the Holy Spirit is active in your daily life?"

"I'm poor, chaste, and obedient for Jesus Christ for the rest of my life, which I hope is a decent push in the right direction." Mind you, when I mentioned poverty I thought of my mother, who, on seeing the splendor of Jesuit real estate for the first time, said, "If this is what poverty looks like, I'd like to see chastity."

CHURCH

The trouble with some Christians is that they want the Holy Spirit to be reduced to external signs. We know, however, from the first Pentecost, and from our own experience, that the Spirit works more subtly, in both unpredictable and ordinary ways. The Holy Spirit seems to specialize in "expect the unexpected."

Pentecost faith challenges us to focus on what the Spirit is doing in our own lives. It's often a case of keeping up with her and following her lead. For most of us the traces of the Holy Spirit are more clearly seen retrospectively. In John's account of the first Pentecost, the primary gift that the Holy Spirit bestows on the disciples is not an external gift but an internal one: peace. Have you noticed how, these days, when we meet someone and ask how they are, they often reply, self-importantly, "Busy," or "Frantic," or "Run off my feet." But, curiously, just as we all compete to be the busiest person we know, we protest that what we really want is "some peace and quiet."

Sometimes, we imagine that peace and quiet means sitting in the lotus position in a darkened room. Christ's gift of peace is more robust than this. Peace is like all the best things in life: a habit born of consistently making good choices. Some people can get through a large amount of work and remain quite serene. Peace, for them, is an attitude of mind and a way of living acquired through patient practice.

Seneca, the first-century Stoic philosopher, observed that his richest and most powerful friends were those who most lacked peace. In *On Anger*, he concluded that they were agitated because they had unreasonable expectations about the smoothness of their life, thinking that their money and power would ensure their comfort and security. When they didn't, they became the angriest of all. If we want to achieve peace of mind, we must have realistic expectations and factor in the things that might go wrong.

Pope Francis has often reminded us that patient listening involves humility and staring down our pride. These associations are out of St. Ignatius of Loyola's playbook.

Today, we would call proud people, in the sense that Ignatius uses the term, control freaks, trying to control everyone and everything for their benefit, or to their will. For Ignatius, the spiritual quest is about staring down the seductive side of these things and reclaiming wealth, beauty, status, intellect, and power as gifts given by God to be used for the coming of Christ's kingdom. Note that he did not reject these elements in our lives. He was smarter than that. He recrafts them for higher and better purposes.

Ignatius thought that in the spiritual life there are three types of people: the first is the one who lives from desire to desire, not caring about God one way or another; the second is the person who wants to attend to their spiritual journey but their bad habits, negative attitudes, and vanity get in the road of making much progress; the last type is the one whose genuine desire is to follow God and live a life of faith, hope, and love. Each of these "types" represents a stage, through which we all too often move in and out, and back and forth.

To keep the momentum going in the right direction, Ignatius encourages us to deepen our humility. The spiritual concept of humility has had a bad rap. It does not mean feeling bad about oneself. The word comes from the Latin *humus*, meaning "close to the earth," and a good way to start being truly humble is to fight against a sense of entitlement and simply be grateful for everything. We did not create the world; we inherited it and, as a start, that should make us profoundly grateful. Keeping it real! Ignatius thought there were three degrees of humility: the first degree is found in a person who lives a good life so as to attain heaven; the second degree is a person who lives a good life in order to bring faith, hope, and love to bear in our world in a way that liberates others as it has liberated that person; finally, there are those who want to be like Christ in every way, serving the poor and being a prophet, and prepared to take rejection and insults so as to point to a greater love.

Careful listening is a more contemplative activity, where we receive before we give. Attentive listening gives dignity to others and honors their experience. In this process, we discover the Holy Spirit's ongoing insight into revelation through hearing the experience of others. No wonder this Pentecost gift is at the heart of Pope Francis's idea of synodality: "A synodal Church is a Church that listens, that realizes that listening 'is more than simply hearing.' It is a mutual listening in which everyone has something to learn."[1]

May we be open to the Holy Spirit as she continued to prepare us for mission by being more peaceful in talking less and honing our ears.

---

1. Pope Francis, address at the ceremony commemorating the fiftieth anniversary of the institution of the Synod of Bishops, October 17, 2015, https://www.vatican.va.

2

LISTENING TO THE CHURCH

There are two Pentecost traditions in the Gospels. The first one, in John 20, has Jesus bequeath the Spirit on the same day as the resurrection. Then, in Acts 2, we have the vivid version that is celebrated in our liturgical calendar. The word *Pentecost* comes from the Greek word *pentēkostē*, meaning "fiftieth." The word *Pentecost* is first found in the Old Testament and was given to the Feast of Weeks, Shavuot, which fell on the fiftieth day after the Passover. Christians celebrate Pentecost on the fiftieth day after Easter Sunday and at the end of the seventh week.

Numbers matter in the Bible. In the Old Testament, the number fifty was the year of jubilee because it was rare for people to live beyond their fiftieth birthday. Three score and ten, seventy, is a huge age in the Bible: very few people ever got there. Once in every lifetime, Israel marked a year of celebration. Of the many features of a Jubilee Year, three were consistent: slaves were set free;

debts were canceled; and fields for crops were allowed to lie fallow. This meant that there was no such thing as lifetime slavery among the Israelites; they aimed for no cross-generational poverty; and they cared for the environment.

What Christians celebrate on Pentecost Sunday is that the power of the Spirit is unleashed on us because we have been set free from the slavery of our sin by Christ, all our debts have been forgiven in Christ, and we have been re-created through Christ. At Pentecost, we celebrate our lives as free sons and daughters of God, a people who forgive as we have been forgiven, and who care for the God's creation.

The second element of the story in Acts 2 is equally challenging. If you're like me you will have been taught that the most public gift on display at the first Pentecost was that a tongue of fire rested on each of the apostles; they were filled with the Holy Spirit and had the ability to speak in different languages. But a more careful reading of the story reveals that the gift received that day was not only one of speaking, but equally one of hearing. Luke, the author of Acts, recounts how the crowds who gathered to hear the apostles were amazed and perplexed, and asked, "How is it that in our own languages we hear them speaking about God's deeds of power?" (see Acts 2:11). Not only was the gift of tongues given to the earliest disciples, but their hearers received "the gift of ears."

When it comes to listening in the Church today, some people mistake mono for stereo, uniformity for unity. At the first Pentecost, the earliest Christians had no such difficulty; they knew that speaking the same language was not what mattered: it was the ability to listen carefully, and to hear the gospel being spoken in different languages. The first Christians were a very complex and diverse bunch. Like the Church today, they had great struggles to deal with, both inside and outside the community. Within a few years of the first Pentecost, there were fierce disagreements between Peter and Paul over Jewish and Gentile converts. Some were for Paul; others were for Apollos. Some died for the faith while others betrayed their Christian brothers and sisters to the authorities. The earliest Christian community was not a utopia.

Pentecost faith holds that while we build our faith on that of the believers who have gone before us, we also have a responsibility to listen to our contemporary culture and to bring it into dialogue with the gospel. That's why courage is one of the Holy Spirit's preeminent gifts. We are not asked to retreat from the world. We are sent out to dialogue with it, affirming what we see to be good, and unashamedly standing over against whatever we see demeans, oppresses, or is life-denying.

This is why we should ask the Holy Spirit to hone our ears as well as to prepare our tongues, so that we may be equipped to hear and discern as well as to proclaim the gospel of Christ in the marketplaces of our own day and age. To talk of the things of God in an increasingly secular world requires prudence and wisdom; we must listen before we speak.

Toward the end of Acts 2, we hear a list of the marks of the first followers of Jesus that is as extraordinary now as it was then. If we take Christ's Spirit as our own, then we too will be filled with awe and open to signs and wonders; we too will sell our possessions and distribute the proceeds to those who need them most; we too will be filled with praise for how God works in and through

9

CHURCH

the world; we too will discover Christ's presence in the "breaking of the bread"; and we too will be joined every day by others wanting to share our joy and fellowship. If we live this out with courage, prudence, and wisdom, then we too will be re-created and will renew the face of the earth.

3

THE SECOND VATICAN COUNCIL

A story told about the last days of Pope John XXIII, even if apocryphal, is instructive about the Church at that time. On June 1, 1963, the Vatican stated that the pope had the flu and asked for our prayers. On June 2, we were told that the pope was in bed and very ill. By June 3, it was announced that he had died of cancer. At least officially, the Holy Father's demise had been very quick indeed. We now know that he had been battling a stomach carcinoma for eight months, with the associated dramatic weight loss that accompanies it. Without telling us, this genial and generous man had been dying before our eyes.

When Pope John Paul II was beatified, John XXIII he announced that his feast day would not be the day of Papa Roncalli's death but October 11, the anniversary of the opening day of the Second Vatican Council, which he had convoked. It was an inspired decision. One of the many guiding principles John hoped would guide the Council was the saying that he quoted in his 1959 encyclical, *Ad Petri Cathedram*: "In essentials, unity; in doubtful matters, liberty; in all things, charity" (72). I wonder what he would make of us now. Except that a saint cannot be unhappy in heaven, John XXIII would surely be rolling in his grave.

The petulant critics snapping at Pope Francis seem to have as their motto, "In all matters, unity; in doubtful matters, hostility; in no things, charity." I note that, from 1978 to 2013, these same cardinals, bishops, theologians, and laypeople now throwing stones at the pope were often the ones who sternly lectured the rest of us that the litmus test of one's Catholic orthodoxy was public fidelity to the teaching of the Holy Father. How things have changed—for them; the rest of us continue to remain loyal to the See of Peter.

Some of Pope Francis's detractors even cast doubt about the validity of his election. Apparently, either the Holy Spirit abandoned the cardinal electors on March 12, 2013, or she never entered the conclave in the first place. So much for trusting the Lord's promise that he would never abandon his Church until the end of time; apparently that only works out if I get the pope I want.

During previous pontificates, I remember being warned against the grave sin of "scandalizing and confusing the faithful." I move in very wide circles and can attest to Pope Francis's extraordinary gift of inspiring faith, hope, and love in believer and unbeliever alike, in sharp contrast to the nasty taste left by the ugly language of online character assassins, the pompous demands for yes or no answers by dubious cardinals, and the pious claims of theologians that they feel forced to point out the pope's errors "out of charity." Could anyone imagine what would have happened to people whose charity impelled them to behave in similar ways toward St. John Paul II or Benedict XVI? Honest, open, respectful disagreement: yes, of course. We edge closer to the truth through arguments between friends. But as one of Christ's faithful, I am confused and scandalized by these arrogant and sanctimonious stone throwers.

Such people don't care about the schismatic tendencies they are encouraging. They argue that "error has no rights," which masks an inclination to a creeping infallibility that forecloses debate on issues about which there is legitimate disagreement. This has serious pastoral fallout at the grassroots of our Church. One gets the sense that their doctrinal edifice is very shaky indeed—give any ground on anything, and the whole house of cards will come tumbling down. The bottom line for Christians is that every person has rights, even those who hold what we might believe is an erroneous position: the right to dignity, respect, charity, and being listened to and interpreted with generosity. If we fail to honor these rights, the evil one is certainly not far away.

Without changing a single jot of essential Catholic doctrine, Pope Francis challenges us all to reflect on the complexity of every life, the struggles everyone faces, and everyone's need for God's mercy. He invites the Church to look afresh at its pastoral practice and its teaching on peace, social justice, and the environment in the light of Scripture, theology, and tradition, the "signs of the times," and the best science and psychology.

This of course is just what John XXIII asked of Vatican II. And he and Paul VI were each to discover that there were powerful forces in the Church filled with fear of change and frightened about where it would all end. These forces were prepared to do anything to stifle reform, to halt and reverse the work of the Council. The present bitter brawling in the Church shows that the struggle to bring the unfinished work of Vatican II to fruition has reached a new crisis point. St John XXIII pray for us.

4

CELIBACY REVISITED

For all the current hostility toward religion in Western nations—some of it entirely justified—Christmas is a hardy annual that keeps on giving to all of us.

When the final report of the Australian Royal Commission, released on December 15, 2017, laid bare the systematic, criminal dysfunctionality of the Catholic Church regarding child sexual abuse and its cover-up, countless priests wondered if anyone would turn up for Christmas Mass. I thought that the report would have a devastating impact on people wanting to celebrate Christmas Mass, and especially bringing their children. I was wrong. In our Jesuit parish of North Sydney, all seven Masses were full, some to bursting and especially the ones dedicated to children and young adults. These were overflowing congregations—onto the steps and the lawns outside. The reasons for this annual pilgrimage for many Catholics are multiple and varied, but among the best reasons are that most of the laity can work out what they want, that they trust the reforms already initiated and the more radical ones to come, and that these despicable crimes do not define the entire community.

I am not sure how any priest in Australia could have presided at Christmas Mass and not have mentioned the victims, survivors, and their families. I am told some avoided it with ease—liturgy and life were clearly not coming together at Christmas in some parishes. It is the time that we can do the greatest good for the greatest number. In our parish, we simply recognized the people, the issues, and prayed for genuine reform of the Church. Everyone was grateful.

One of the criticisms of the Royal Commission is that it unduly focused on the Catholic Church. I did not realize that the Commission never looked at government schools, the Muslim community, or at media and entertainment organizations. That now looks very odd indeed. However, while the Commission restated that the most common place where a child is sexually abused is, by far, the family home, the figures involving the Church point to a shocking institutional culture.

The Commission heard about 10,661 allegations and have already referred 2,559 cases to the police. Of the total number of allegations, 4,418 of them relate to Catholic institutions. Since 1950, as many as 384 Catholic diocesan priests, 188 priests belonging to religious orders, 597 brothers, and 96 sisters have had claims of child sexual abuse made against them.

All but two of the recommendations of the Commission have been welcomed by the Catholic Church. The major ones include uniform laws in every jurisdiction regarding child protection; a National Working with Children Register and wider professional disclosure laws; an

Office of Child Safety, which will independently investigate and determine accusations of and issues around abuse and assess compensation; and a federal redress scheme where victims receive a maximum of $150,000 each, not as compensation but as a recognition of their incalculable suffering. The Commission estimates that this scheme will cost $4.3 billion over ten years, with religious and other private institutions required to contribute $2.4 billion.

The Commission targets the Vatican on a score of canonical and other procedures, and not surprisingly, two suggestions captured the media's imagination: an end to compulsory celibacy for diocesan clergy—not because it claimed that celibacy causes abuse, but because of the secretive clerical culture it fosters—and that the seal of confession should not apply to revelations of child sexual abuse, and that "absolution can and should be withheld until they [the abusers] report themselves to civil authorities."

Most Western Catholics would welcome the change to mandatory celibacy for priests. The seal of confession is a different matter. Egregious as this specific crime is, a valid argument could be made for a host of other despicable crimes as well, rape, for example, or domestic violence. While I do not doubt that historically this sacrament has been abused, very few people attend it now, and the truth is, the attention it is receiving is disproportionate to the impact a change would make to the protection of children. I could imagine some extreme activists confessing this crime to see what the priest or bishop would do. Some clergy might decide to exclude themselves from hearing confessions at all. Already some (religious order) priests only do weddings, baptisms, and funerals for friends and family. Furthermore, I cannot find a recommendation by the Commission that disclosures of abuse made to journalists or lawyers should be included in mandatory reporting—a point that seems inconsistent.

Francis Sullivan, the CEO of the Church's Truth, Justice and Healing Council, has observed, "People say the Church needs to get its house back in order; but I say we have to rebuild the house." This Christmas proved again that Catholics are hardy, being given every reason to walk away and take their children with them. Thank God that their first instinct is not to cut and run because, in the rebuilding of Christ's Church, which we love, we have never needed these people more.

5

EVANGELIZATION

Few people have seized the imagination of their own and subsequent generations of Catholics in the same way that St. Francis Xavier has. His feast day is December 3.

Among his other many outstanding gifts, he was an indiscriminate baptizer. It is unknown how many people Xavier baptized. Some of his biographers guess that the figure is somewhere between forty to one hundred thousand believers. One of his letters from India states that on one day he performed four thousand baptisms; that's 167 an hour. I am guessing those ceremonies weren't all that personal. Indeed, he may have been a sacramental forerunner to Rev. Sun Myung Moon.

Xavier's christening prowess was such that, when Rome could not recover his whole body, the Jesuit General Claudio Acquaviva ordered Francis Xavier's baptizing right arm to be severed at the elbow and conveyed to Rome. In 1617, it was enshrined there in the Jesuit Church of the Gesù. This bejeweled and rather ghoulish relic (by our standards today) is still there for all to see.

CHURCH

Xavier's mission to baptize was about giving everyone a chance at salvation. He would be appalled by the attitude of some clergy these days who demand of young parents a strong commitment to and practice of the faith, and that they turn up to several preparation classes before they can get their babies baptized.

While I am all for the good order of sacraments and appropriate preparation for them, my attitude mirrors more that of Xavier's: I baptize anything that moves; I marry anything that moves; and I bury anything that doesn't.

Making preparation courses an absolute condition for baptism is a contravention of canon 868, where the only grounds for "delaying," not denying, the sacrament is where the celebrant knows there is no hope that a child will be brought up in the Catholic religion. These cases should be extremely rare.

Pope Francis recently told a group of newly ordained priests, "It is never necessary to refuse baptism to someone who asks for it!"

So, I think we should recover Francis Xavier's practices regarding baptism. While we would do so for very different theological and pastoral reasons, there remains a critical element to his missionary style that we would do well to recover in our personal and communal evangelization.

Xavier actually got off his backside and went out to the world. Today, the Church can often act as though we have every right to sit at home and wait for the world to come to us—often expecting it to talk our talk and walk our walk before having much to do with it.

The problem with this approach is that when we ponder the great commission of Mark (16:12) and its parallels, Jesus doesn't tell the disciples to wait at home for the throng to come to them, but to do what Xavier did: go out and meet the world where they are—as they are.

Sometimes, I am invited to speak at evangelization conferences, and I listen to other speakers expound platforms and programs of faith renewal. Many of these are worthy to be sure. Personally, I like the paradox that our biggest moments of intersecting with the real world are when they come to us, at least partly on our terms. Baptisms, weddings, and funerals are three of the greatest tools for evangelization that we have.

These days, most of those who gather do not darken the Church's door except on these three occasions. Some bring with them deep wounds inflicted by Church personnel. All come with a vulnerability that only sorrow and joy can open.

Imagine if our liturgies on these occasions were as welcoming and generous as they were well prepared? Imagine if the first words the congregation heard from the celebrant were of compassion and inclusion? In my pastoral experience, this can be the beginning of a new evangelization.

I want to be as welcoming of people who do not necessarily tick all the religious boxes because the Lord seems to have held a special affection for them—non-temple-going shepherds, Jewish tax collectors, women with bad reputations, notorious sinners with whom he dined, lepers and those who were considered ritually unclean. He didn't ask them to do a mandatory four-week program. Only a very few of these became his public disciples. Tradition holds that they all became his followers in their own ways. So, if this was good enough for the Lord, then why would his approach not be good enough for us?

Like Francis Xavier, we need to recover the most ancient tradition to the sacraments: it doesn't matter where you start in the life of faith, it matters where Christ will finish it.

6

READING THE SIGNS

At the start of Advent 1992, I was appointed to the parish within the red-light district of Sydney and promptly refounded the church choir. The first chorister to apply was a very tall, beautifully dressed woman who approached me after Mass and said in her *basso profundo*, "Father, my name's Gloria, and I sing bass."

"It's always hard to find basses," I said. "See you tomorrow night for our first rehearsal."

As Gloria walked away, she stopped, turned, and said, "You realize I'm a trannie don't ya, Father?"

"Yes, Gloria. Even I had figured that one out. It's unusual to find a woman who can sing bass."

Gloria was, without question, the worst bass I have ever heard in my life, but word about her spread like wildfire throughout Kings Cross, and soon, many of her friends were coming to Mass to see and hear her sing. One Sunday, at the end of a hymn, Gloria let go of a big

CHURCH

"AHH-MEN" and soon there were two pews of transvestites on their feet yelling out, "You show 'em, girl."

However, not everyone in the parish was coping!

Eventually, the issue came before the parish council. Just as they were about to vote on whether Gloria should be asked to leave the choir, my Irish-born Jesuit parish priest spoke up. "You know," he said, "Jesus was always strong on 'reading the signs.' Maybe, just maybe, Gloria is a sign to us this Advent that God's gifts do not always come to us in little neat boxes, and that God comes to afflict the comfortable, and comfort the afflicted. But," he concluded, "I could be wrong, so go ahead and have your vote." We won the vote! Gloria remained.

After six months, Gloria told me that her wife was dying of cancer in another city and that she needed help to face up to her issues and return home. While undergoing counseling, she vanished from the parish. Then, one day, a man turned up on my doorstep. I did not know who it was until he spoke. "G'day, Father, it's Gordon, and I've just come to say goodbye."

A good while later a letter arrived from Gordon:

I just want you to know that last night at home, my wife died peacefully of the breast cancer she's had for the last eighteen months. After the undertakers took her away and I put our boys back to bed, I was overwhelmed to think I wouldn't have been here if it wasn't for the goodness of the parish at Kings Cross. I know it wasn't easy for some of you having a drag queen in the choir, but you believed in me even when I didn't know who I was, what I wanted and where I needed to go. Who could have thought that singing at Mass was eventually going to play itself out into reconciling a husband to a wife, who was such a model of forgiveness, and giving back to two boys their dad, because they've done nothing to deserve to be orphans. I'm not sure if you're aware how often you sing of and preach about "amazing grace." Never stop doing that. I am a witness to its power. And if I understand it correctly, amazing grace says it doesn't matter where you start; it matters where God's love can finish it.

At the start of Advent, we are encouraged to walk in the light, to be armed by it, and to get good at reading the signs. May this Advent enable us to realize afresh that the signs of God rarely arrive in little neat boxes, and that through amazing grace, we should expect the unexpected by journey's end.

PART TWO

LITURGY AND SACRAMENTS

7

A EUCHARISTIC PASSPORT

A eucharistic passport! First, I thought it must be a joke, but then, I soon discovered it was anything but, and that wasn't isolated to one eccentric parish priest. The idea is catching on, big time.

It starts from the best of intentions. Many priests are worried about the increasing lack of attendance of Catholic children at Mass, especially those preparing for the sacraments. This is not a new phenomenon, and it applies equally to children who attend Catholic schools and those who go elsewhere.

So, some priests now require children to prove that they have attended several Masses before they are able to receive the sacraments of reconciliation, Eucharist, and confirmation.

The biblical number twelve seems to be emerging as the agreed number of mandated Masses. The children must get their passports, which often carry a photo, signed and dated by the priest at the end of Mass. One priest demanded that all twelve Masses had to be in his parish, but when three-quarters of the prospective candidates failed to fulfill this requirement, he relented and issued visas permitting them to travel to other parishes. It's still not working.

Priests have got this idea from another canonically illegal act—making attendance at baptismal preparation classes an absolute prerequisite for that sacrament. I entirely support the best preparation possible for every sacrament, and I have seen how these sessions can be the beginning of the renewal of faith, but it's wrong to make attendance at these classes mandatory. Canon 868 states that the only grounds for the denial of infant baptism is where there is no hope that the child will be brought up in the Catholic religion. That's very rare. And even then, canon law states that, in these cases, baptism is not to be refused but to be "deferred." In fact, Pope Francis emphatically told a group of newly ordained priests that "it is never necessary to refuse baptism to someone who asks for it!"[1]

The same concern and unease apply to this new fashion for demanding proof of attendance at a certain number of Masses for a Catholic child to qualify for access to other sacraments. While I share the frustration among priests in seeing faces of children whom they barely recognize rolling up to Church for their first holy communion, it is an abuse of clerical power to exclude children from the sacramental life of the Church unless they have fulfilled a locally invented requirement. It is against the letter and their spirit of canon 213, which

---

1. Pope Francis, Homily, "Holy Mass with Priestly Ordinations," April 26, 2015.

states that the faithful "have the right to receive assistance from the sacred pastors out of the spiritual goods of the Church, especially the word of God and the Sacraments."

While canon 777 gives the parish priest the responsibility for ensuring the catechesis of children and young people in his parish, other canons make it clear that this responsibility is not executed in isolation and that the local bishop can delegate Catholic school teachers and other qualified people to prepare children for the sacraments. Participation at Mass is the best preparation for the sacraments, but we should not be pushed into the pastorally dangerous situation of insisting, "No Mass; no sacraments." This can have unforeseen and potentially tragic consequences.

I know a Buddhist father whose Catholic wife died in a car accident and who is raising their eight-year-old twins. They attend the local Catholic school. He is now effectively forced to attend Mass twelve times this year because he will not send them to church on their own. That's a breach of canon law. I have heard of a struggling single mother who has a second weekend job that is twenty-five miles (forty kilometers) from her home and the local parish. The family stays with her atheist father, who refuses to take his grandchildren to Mass. Because the exhausted mother does not get back in time to attend the local 6:00 p.m. Sunday night Mass with her children, her eldest daughter was excluded from making her first holy communion. Then there is the father who as an altar boy was abused by a priest and forced to return to the scene of the crime twelve times last year. He felt retraumatized by the abuse of power that forced him to do this for his children. He refuses to speak to the local priest.

We want people at Mass who are drawn there by love, not driven there by fear. Of course, we must encourage and invite everyone to Sunday Mass and make the liturgy engaging, inclusive, welcoming, and hospitable. Whenever possible, parishes should have an appropriately adapted liturgy for children. And we should teach them why the Mass matters, primarily by showing not telling, in the way we live it during the week.

But these are Christ's sacraments, not ours: Christ invites and hosts and missions us at every Mass, and the primary law of Christ is to love God, our neighbor, and ourselves; and there is not only one way to do any of these three. Indeed, as God's grace works individually with every heart, we are drawn to all the sacraments as they sustain us on the greatest of all journeys—to eternal life—where the only stamp required is the one that expresses how well we have loved.

8

CELEBRATING CHRIST'S FORGIVENESS

The third rite of reconciliation enjoyed a great reception in many places in Australia until November 1998. That month, seven metropolitan archbishops together with the chairman and secretaries of several national bishops' conference committees attended a synod in Rome with various prefects of Vatican dicasteries. At the end of the synod, a document, the "Statement of Conclusions," was produced and signed. The tone of it was generally negative, and the lax administration of the sacrament of penance received special attention.

The bishops were told that the first and second rites of penance were the "sole ordinary means" by which Catholics are sacramentally forgiven by God and that general absolution (the third rite of reconciliation) was "illegitimate" and had to be "eliminated." All this hit headlines around the country.

LITURGY AND SACRAMENTS

In December 1999, I remember meeting an Anglican bishop who laughed as he said, "You Roman Catholics are the only group of Christians I know who can gather a church filled with confessing believers on a Tuesday night to repent explicitly of their sins and receive God's forgiveness and send them home because they wanted to use the wrong rite. We Anglicans would be grateful that so many had gathered for the single purpose of celebrating God's unbounded mercy."

I recently suggested that the third rite of reconciliation should become the parish norm to protect vulnerable priests and bishops from the increasingly common practice of activists trying to entrap them through legal requirement of disclosing child sexual abuse heard in confession. It set off a minor fire storm. Some rightly said that the communal rite should return, and not as a means to avoid being charged by the police. Others took me to task for even suggesting that this form of Christ's forgiveness was remotely equal in efficacy to the other two rites. From my own graced experience of the first and second rites, as well as the privilege at presiding over both forms for decades, I need no convincing of their beauty and power when they are celebrated well. However, questioning the motivation of those who seek the third rite and even suggesting that it is does not deliver on its sacramental promise of Christ's forgiveness is dangerous stuff.

One priest attached to his email a statement from his bishop, where it was claimed the third rite was more about confessing "sinfulness" than sins. The bishop should have attended some of the communal rites I've been to where the relationship between the general and the particular was acutely felt. The bishop's letter went on to denigrate the third rite as a "do-it-yourself" parody of the sacrament. This commentary is as tragic as it is ill-considered.

I cannot see what is sacramental DIY about gathering in a church at a nominated time for the specific reason of celebrating that Christ's forgiveness is greater than our sins; hearing the word of God and a homily; performing an examination of conscience; making an act of contrition and purpose of amendment; kneeling to receive sacramental absolution, and then being absolved by Christ through the ministrations of the priest or bishop; saying the Lord's Prayer; and then being blessed and sent in peace while singing of the mercy of the Lord. All of this is celebrated in the context of knowing that, if a particular penitent were carrying a mortal, or deadly, sin, then that person is further required to attend to the first rite of reconciliation.

In advocating one form of penance to the exclusion of others, we need to be careful that we are not seen to be more interested in social control than in how the Lord's mercy works through us, in us, with us, and without us.

The reality is that for all our preaching, teaching, demands, and encouragement, since the third rite was eliminated after November 1998, the vast majority of Australian Catholics do not access any form of penance, ever. Even Lenten and Advent penance services have noticeably shrunk in recent years. If we believe in the *sensus fidei*, then the people of God have not received the teaching that the communal rite of penance is "illegitimate." For almost thirty years we have chosen form over substance, and the Body of Christ is weaker for it.

LITURGY AND SACRAMENTS

Though it is only anecdotal, I believe that if we restored the more ancient communal rite of penance, we could regularly see again a Church full of confessing Catholics repenting of their sins and of celebrating God's unbounded mercy. Other than an institutional back down, where would the downside be?

9

THE SACRAMENTS ARE FOR THE PEOPLE

If he can make 'em, he can break 'em.

Like every pope since the high medieval period, Pope Francis has three different functionary powers: he is supreme teacher, pastor, and legislator of the Catholic Church. The last category doesn't usually attract much attention except from bishops, some clerics, and canon lawyers, whose job it is to keep up with the legislative agenda of every pope.

This situation suddenly changed, however, during a papal flight between Iquique and Santiago in Chile. Flight attendants Paula Podest Ruiz and Carlos Ciuffardi Elorriga asked Francis to "bless" their civil union. Years before, they had planned a Catholic wedding ceremony but, on the day of their wedding, an earthquake struck, and their church collapsed.

LITURGY AND SACRAMENTS

Being the good and supreme pastor he is, the pope asked some more questions and discovered that they had two daughters. Francis not only offered to "bless" their marriage but to marry them in the Catholic Church: what is technically called a retroactive convalidation—"a radical sanation"—which sounds like a nasty medical procedure.

Carlos later told reporters on the plane that the pope had asked him, "Do you want me to marry you? Are you sure?" He and Paula had both replied, "Yes, of course." And with the president of LATAM airlines acting as the witness, the cylinder in the sky became a chapel of love. It was, indeed, a marriage made in heaven.

While a pope cannot change divine (natural) law or received Catholic teaching—the creeds, for example—he can change almost any other ecclesiastical law he likes, because he has supreme, full, and immediate legal powers, answerable to God alone. If he wants to, "he can make 'em, and he can break 'em."

The pope has been criticized on all sides for this high-flying wedding. Some suggesting it was a pastoral stunt, "pastoral populism" in the words of one usually supportive commentator. The more canonically minded have not held back. Where was the paperwork with all the necessary investigations and declarations? Because the couple were officially living in sin, did the pope hear their confessions first? In what diocese did the wedding occur and where is it registered? Where was the pastoral emergency for such a radical solution? Where was the second witness? Where were the required liturgical vestments? Where was the Dispensation from Canonical Form regarding marrying a couple outside of an actual Church?

Two days later, the backstory was revealed on the pope's return flight from Peru to Rome. The wedding had not been as spontaneous as first thought. The groom had attended the pope on an internal flight the previous day, and it was then that he had told Francis his story, and asked if he would bless his marriage the next day, when he knew that his fiancée would also be working as an attendant.

The pope explained to the reporters who were traveling on the flight with him, "One of you said I was crazy to do this. I judged they were prepared; they knew what they were doing. Both of them had prepared before God—with the sacrament of penance—and I married them....Otherwise they could have put it off for another ten years." He concluded with the reminder, "The sacraments are for the people."

Alas, on the ground, some deacons and priests are still dealing with bishops who use canon and liturgical law like weapons in their ideological fights, which all too often sacrifice pastoral care on the altar of narrow legalism. And though I know there are many good people working in marriage tribunals, there are still too many stories of painful delays and of hurtful and occasionally damaging exchanges being experienced by individuals (often the non-Catholic party) and families during the nullity process.

There are even some bishops who have failed to implement the changes to the annulment process the Holy Father announced in December 2015. These included a provision for a "fast-track" annulment when there was a clear case for a declaration of nullity, an instruction that the annulment process should be provided gratis (and not require a "donation"), and a new guideline that, where both the parties were seeking a declaration of nullity, the matter should normally be settled one way or the other within 120 days. But although the pope might imagine he is the only one who can pick and choose the canons he likes...not all bishops seem to take the same view.

I am delighted for Paula and Carlos and their daughters. I just wish I had the power "to make 'em and break 'em" like Francis. In many countries, only a fraction of young Catholics bothers with a sacramental marriage at all. When the ones that do are confronted by a tussle between a merciful pastoral outcome and the letter of canon law, Pope Francis's reminder that "the sacraments are for the people" is all too often forgotten.

10

MARTYRS AND SAINTS

In medieval England, All Saints' Day was known as All Hallows' Day. We don't use the word *hallowed* very much except in the Lord's Prayer; in All Hallows' Eve, or "Halloween"; and in the formal way we refer to "hallowed ground," or to a "hallowed institution." The word was given a makeover for a younger audience in 2007, when the final novel in the Harry Potter series, *Harry Potter and the Deathly Hallows*, was published, and then sold 65 million copies. J. K. Rowling tells her readers that the three deathly hallows are the Elder Wand, the Resurrection Stone, and the Cloak of Invisibility. Whoever owns all three hallows gains mastery over death, and so we start to see the relationship between Rowling's text and the mystical traditions she has inherited.

On All Hallows' Day, we celebrate the memory of the holy ones in heaven with God. The three pathways to being declared a saint are heroic virtue, mysticism, and martyrdom. In the last category, there are four subdivisions: white martyrdom, where you are persecuted for the faith, but never shed blood; green martyrdom, where you do extreme penance and fasting for the love of God; red martyrdom, where you are killed for the faith; and the most recent category, introduced, in 2017, by Pope Francis, a martyr of charity, where you die as a result of putting yourself at risk in the service of others.

The first people honored as saints by the earliest Christians were martyrs. The word *martyr* comes from the word *witness*. In fact, All Saints' Day, celebrated throughout the Church on the first day of November, has its roots in the early Church's Martyrs' Day, attested to by a hymn written in 359 by St. Ephraim. The name was changed to All Saints' Day in the seventh century.

Our Christian foremothers and forefathers counted themselves blessed to suffer and die as Jesus suffered and died. Indeed, the requirement that a child being baptized must have godparents comes from the time of Christian persecution. Those who had left their Jewish or Gentile families to join the Christian community knew they might be martyred for their faith; to ensure that their children would not be returned to their non-Christian extended families, they would ask other Christians in God's name to swear they would take them into their homes and raise them as their own in the event of their deaths. A godparent was honored to raise the children of those persecuted for the kingdom of heaven.

Prophets and martyrs are often linked. They are put to death because they cannot live any other way. Such is the liberty of spirit, thirst for justice, and witness to truth they embody: they threaten the social and religious leaders of their time and place to such an extent that they have to be silenced.

The glorification of suffering and martyrdom can attract fanatics. As uncomfortable as it is for Christians to admit, some of our martyrs did not die with the healthiest of religious motivations. We only have to read their letters to discover that some actively went looking for death: longing and praying that "the crown of martyrdom" would be granted to them. Paradise awaited. There is an important distinction between being killed because of one's faith and zealously seeking to die; between being martyred and being on a suicide mission.

A saint is someone whom the Church believes is in heaven with God. When we declare that someone has been "canonized" (in Latin: *canonizare*, "admit to the authoritative list"), we are saying that, because of the way they lived their Christian lives, God could not deny them heaven, so they have to be added to the roster of recognized saints. Wrongly, we often think that saints are perfect, but in fact, their greatest witness is how they coped with the difficulties of life, and how they reflected the love of God in a variety of ways.

We hallow what God has done through them because we hope to join them. St. Paul thought saints were everywhere. I think he was right, canonized or otherwise. For most of us, sanctity and martyrdom will not come dramatically. The daily routine of looking after a sick child or spouse or elderly parent, or of living with a mental, physical, emotional, or spiritual illness, or bearing the scourge of being unemployed, homeless, or addicted, or being unable to shake off the feeling that we are unlovable:

they all bring with them the reality of sharing in the lot of the martyrs and the saints.

This is the holy cloud of witnesses who saw God in this world and are now fully alive to him in the next, cheering us on in this life and all the way to the next.

11

JESUS, A DIFFERENT SUPERHERO

During a recent Q&A in a Catholic school, I asked the fourth graders who Jesus was for them. One bright young lad said, "Jesus is so cool. He's better than Superman."

No one in the class laughed or looked bemused at this suggestion. "I don't think so," I said, but before I could explain further, the young theologian excitedly interrupted me. "No, you're right, Father," he said. "Jesus was human, so he is more like Batman or Iron Man, only better." In the circumstances, having Christ come out as the best of the superhero bunch might be counted as a win.

It should not surprise us that this genre now forms the theological paradigm within which the story of Jesus is often understood by young Catholics. The Marvel superhero franchise is now one of the biggest at the cinema. Though they have been popular since they first appeared in comic books in 1939, since the film *Iron Man* was released in 2008, we cannot get enough of *Captain America, Thor, Iron Man, Wolverine, Spider-Man, X-Men*, the *Fantastic Four*, and the *Hulk. The Avengers: Endgame* is now one of the biggest grossing films of all time, having made US$2.8 billion worldwide soon after it opened in April 2019. In fact, there are two hundred different Marvel heroes, so the takeover may have only just begun.

The premise of the superhero is found in Greek philosophy, where the good vigilante restores moral justice. As Aristotle says in *Politics*, "There are men [*sic*], so godlike, so exceptional, that they naturally, by right of their extraordinary gifts, transcend all moral judgment or constitutional control. There is no law which embraces men of that calibre: they are themselves law."

These superhero films may not be to everyone's taste, but many teenagers and young adults are enthralled by them, and they deserve careful analysis. While 18- to 30-year-olds are the least likely demographic to attend Christian worship in developed countries, it does not mean that they are lacking in any interest in the metaphysical. Of the top twenty box-office films of all time, thirteen are about other worlds, other modes of existence, or different forms of beings. Angels and spirits have never had it so good.

At the cinema, young people are contemplating their place in a larger frame of reference, where physical laws count for less and a personal relationship with a metaphysical and, often, a metaethical world, is taken seriously. Whether we like it or not, the multiplex, not the Church, is the context within which an increasing number of people encounter a world of otherness, of ethical systems, personal and social mythologies that transcend the everyday.

In her 1996 book, *Seeing and Believing: Religion and Values in the Movies*, Margaret Miles rightly argues,

> The development of popular film coincided historically and geographically with the emancipation of public life from church control and patronage. "Congregations" became "audiences" as film created a new public sphere in which, under the guise of "entertainment," values are formulated, circulated, resisted, and negotiated. The public sphere is an arena in which various overlapping minorities can converse, contest and negotiate, forming temporary coalitions.

Whatever of the poor catechesis that leads some young Catholics to see Jesus as just another superhero, why has this franchise taken such hold on this generation? It seems the need for a messiah never goes away. Through high rates of unemployment, marriage breakdown, interrupted family life, social dislocation at every level, political chaos, and looming ecological threats, young people want some comfort and reassurance. They want to imagine being saved from the external threats by someone, anyone, who can bring order out of the ongoing disorder that has characterized their young lives.

What worries me especially about these films is the dynamic of passivity that is established between the savior and the saved. The messiah destroys evil and restores balance and hope; the rest of us just need to stay out of the road and watch open mouthed. While we believe that

LITURGY AND SACRAMENTS

Jesus saves us from the forces of evil and destruction, we are not passive in our salvation. Amazing grace might be unearned and undeserved, but it is not forced upon us, because we can reject faith, and hope, and love. We are invited to enjoy the saving love of God in an ongoing relationship with the Father, the Son, and the Holy Spirit that sees us do all that we can to work with them to renew the face of the earth.

12

A PLACE AT THE TABLE

A teacher asked her third graders to draw a picture of the ascension. Not unsurprisingly, most of them did a rather conventional portrait of Jesus rising into the clouds. One of her students, David, who was a particularly gifted artist, had Jesus blasting off into the sky. Down the side of Jesus's white garment were the letters *NASA*. When he displayed his picture to the class, he provided all the sound effects that he imagined must have accompanied Christ's ascension. He concluded his presentation by saying, without a hint of irony, "The ascension must have been a real blast!" All the other kids said in chorus, "Awesome."

None of us can blame David for marrying our modern culture with an ancient story. In fact, if some of us are honest, David's "space-shuttle Jesus" is not far from what we might think as well.

The stories of the ascension, however, are not primarily interested in how or when Jesus got back to heaven.

John and Paul never mention it at all. The accounts of Mark and Matthew have it happening on the same day as the resurrection and Luke's account has it occurring forty days after Easter on the same day as Pentecost.

The one thing about which all the New Testament writers agree is where in heaven Jesus went and where he is presently—at God's right hand.

Even to this day, being on someone's right is a place of honor. Imagine being invited to Buckingham Palace or the White House and finding that you have been placed on the right hand of the king of England or the president of the United States.

In the Old Testament, being on the right hand of David, Samuel, or Elijah was to be the anointed and favored one, the true son or daughter. And it survives in popular culture, too.

Game of Thrones may be too explicit on every level for many people, but it remains the most watched drama ever on subscription television. Of all the characters in this story, the most important person after the reigning monarch is "the Hand of the King." He is regularly just referred to as "the Hand" and wears a coveted pin depicting a hand so as to designate his authority.

In telling us, then, that Jesus is now at God's right hand, the Gospels use shorthand to state that God affirms everything Jesus said and did on earth, and that he therefore is the One for us to follow.

However, in the Gospels, Jesus goes one step further and teaches us that where he is, so shall we be, that he is going to prepare a place for us, and that, in and through him, we will have life and have it to the full.

The Feast of the Ascension is the day, each year, where we remember and we celebrate that, just as Jesus was welcomed to God's right hand, so, too, we may be welcomed to the symbolic right hand of Jesus. This is his promise, this is our faith, and this is the hope we're called to proclaim to the world.

And let's be clear about the invitation. There is nothing we have ever done, are doing, or will do that will get our name removed from the guest list to the feast of God's kingdom. The challenge is accepting that we have a standing invitation and to live lives worthy of the love that got us invited in the first place.

The second piece of shorthand in the ascension stories is the mountaintop. In the Scriptures, almost every time someone goes up a mountain or to the hill country, a significant encounter with God ensues. Mentioned over five hundred times in the Bible, mountains are where people felt close to God and were the locations for conversion, commissioning, and worship.

The ascension is our yearly call to conversion of life and being commissioned to live our baptism in spirit and in truth.

The third piece of shorthand in Luke's account of the ascension concerns the forty days. In the Bible, the number forty is always a time of formation, and so Christ does not send the disciples out cold; rather, he has been preparing them to proclaim that all people now possess the dignity of belonging to the family of God and are invited to sit at the hand of God.

And as we go out to the world, we are given an eternal promise—that Christ abides before us, behind us, over and in us, within and without us, now and forever. I'm not sure we could think of a greater blast that could fill us more with awe.

13

BROKEN AND SHARED, POURED OUT AND SENT

A Protestant friend told me once that he could never contemplate becoming a Roman Catholic "because you are eucharistic cannibals." He was sincere. I was speechless—and that rarely happens.

I always think of that conversation when we come to the feast of the body and blood of Christ. We need to own that, in some popular devotions and pious legends, there can be too explicit a link in the physicality of the Eucharist. We are not Christian cannibals feasting on Jesus's flesh and blood, on his liver, brain, and bones.

The best traditions in the Church are careful in the language they use about how Jesus is present in the Eucharist. When the *Catechism* speaks of the real presence of the Eucharist, it never refers to "Jesus" but always to "Christ." This distinction matters. The Eucharist is a sacrament of Easter.

As a Catholic, I believe that Christ, raised by God from the dead, is fully and truly present to me in the consecrated bread and wine at Mass. St. Paul was at pains to rebut two extreme views about the glorified body of Christ: a crude physicalism, where the glorified body of Christ was simply a resuscitation of his corpse; and an overspiritualization where Christ was raised from the dead was an ethereal ghost (cf. 1 Cor 15).

The *Catechism* puts the issue succinctly: "The glorious body (is) not limited by space and time but able to be present how and when he wills; for Christ's humanity can no longer be confined to earth" (*CCC* 645). The risen body and blood of Christ is found in the experience of Easter, an encounter that transcends the boundaries of human weakness, but at the same time, raises it up and heals all the wounds of the body. The divine presence of Christ lives in and through the redeemed physical world but is not bound or contained by it.

For the first few centuries, Christians adored Christ as they consumed communion. The reservation of the blessed sacrament was rare and then mainly for the sick. From the fifth century, as Christians believed that they were not worthy to receive the Eucharist, their adoration of the risen Lord took the place of communing with him.

The former Feast of Corpus Christi came about in the twelfth century when many Catholics simply never received communion at all but felt close to Christ through the act of adoration. In 1215, the Church had to enact a law, still in force for us today, requiring Catholics to receive communion at least once a year, at Eastertime.

The Second Vatican Council taught that while the act of adoration is important and consistent with the intensity of our love, receiving the risen Lord in holy communion was the more ancient part of our tradition and a more complete act. Indeed, Vatican II also reminded us that, while we believe that Christ is uniquely and intimately present in the bread of life and the cup of salvation, we also believe that Christ's real presence also comes to us in the word of God, in the gathered assembly of God's people, and in the person of the ministers.

Sometimes, a few believers can speak of the Eucharist as a magical act. Jesus counters such a notion by telling us that he gives us himself "for the life of the world." There is an important difference between grace and magic: one is a trick for a show; the other is the power of love, which expresses itself in faith, hope, and service. The Eucharist is not intimate and unique because it is magic. It's not intimate and unique because we only gaze upon the elements. The Eucharist is intimate and unique because ordinary earthly signs of bread and wine are transformed by God's love and consumed in faith. As we eat and drink these elements, Christ becomes part of us, and we come alive in Christ.

In the fifth century, St. Augustine taught his people that, if they truly loved the Eucharist, they would become what they eat. By receiving, into our hands, the bread and wine of Easter at Christ's feast—blessed and broken, poured out and shared—we say "Amen" (literally: "so be it") to becoming the same in Christ: blessed, broken, poured out, and shared in love for the life of the world.

Understood in these ways, the body and blood of Christ moves away from celebrating the static presence of God in the blessed sacrament, to the dynamic living out of this feast in our daily lives. In this way, Corpus Christi becomes the most moveable and radical of feasts.

14

THE MYSTERY OF HOLY WEEK

Every so often, there is a film that haunts you. *Silence* is one of them for me. Not that it's easy watching. True to its title, there is no lush soundtrack to sweep the emotions along. Although the stories are related on many levels, *Silence* is very different from *The Mission*.

Based on Shusaku Endo's 1966 award-winning novel, the drama opens with the 1614 edict in Japan that all foreigners and their colonial influences, especially their religion, are to be expunged.

Word arrives at Macao that Father Christovão Ferreira (Liam Neeson), the Jesuit superior in Japan, has apostatized, converted to Buddhism, and is collaborating with the Japanese government.

Two of Ferreira's Jesuit students, Father Sebastian Rodrigues (Andrew Garfield) and Father Francisco Garupe (Adam Driver), will not believe that their former teacher has defected. They volunteer to go on a secret mission to Japan to find Ferreira and discover the truth. In time, they are tracked down, captured, and tortured.

Even to this day, we can be inspired when we hear of heroic men and women—religious or otherwise—who are prepared to die so that others might live, remain defiant in the face of evil, or give their lives in the service of justice. Martyrs walk the talk and pay the price. We need them, though their witness usually provides an uncomfortable contrast to what we would do in similar circumstances. Most of us come up short.

The problem with martyrdom in any context is that it can attract fanatics. As uncomfortable as it is for Christians to admit, some of our martyrs did not die with the best of religious motivations. We only need to read their letters to discover that they actively went looking for death; longing and praying that "the crown of martyrdom" would be granted to them. Paradise awaited.

While it is all good and well for comfortable believers like me to be critical of those who sacrifice their lives, there is an important distinction between being killed because of one's faith and the justice that it demands, and seeking to die—between being martyred and being on a suicide mission.

What is at stake, here, is a hotly contested theological point in the contemporary academy: how we can understand and appropriate Jesus's sacrifice on Good Friday while also believing that "God is light and in him there is no darkness" (1 John 1:5); that while we hold that God *permits* evil in the world, we reject that Gods *sends* it or *deals* in it.

The problem is that some traditional readings of Jesus's death can easily give justification to a very few Christians hunting down the martyr's crown because that is what the Father requires.

With all due respect to Saints Paul, Clement of Alexandria, and Anselm of Canterbury, and later John Calvin, many modern believers cannot baldly accept that the perfect God of love set us up for a fall in the Garden, then got so angry with us that the grisly death of his only perfect Son was the only way to repair the breach between us.

This is not the only way into the mystery of Holy Week.

Orthodox theologians may be helpful here in explaining how they see Jesus's death on Good Friday as the price he paid for the way he lived. Rather than ask, "Why did Jesus die?" they suggest it might be even more confronting to ask, "Why was Jesus killed?" This puts the last days of Jesus's suffering and death in an entirely new perspective, where Jesus did not simply and only come to die. Rather, Jesus came to live and because of the courageous and radical way he lived his life, and the saving love he embodied for all humanity, he threatened the political, social, and religious authorities of his day to such an extent that they executed him. But the God of life and love in whom we believe had the last word on Good Friday and Easter Sunday—raising Christ up that we might all be raised to new life in him and through him.

Jesus did not go looking for death on its own terms. It came to him, and he could not and would not resile from it.

LITURGY AND SACRAMENTS

In this light, we can see that we have other options regarding where and how we can find a God of love amid our own particular and personal martyrdoms.

Maybe it's perfect therefore that the film, *Silence*, is set in the land of the rising sun.

15

OUR FIGURATIVE DESERT

There is one school of New Testament scholarship that argues that Jesus did not just go to the desert and pay John the Baptist a visit, but that he could have been his disciple for some time and later made a break from him. In the Gospels, John the Baptist emerges as a fierce character, opting out of towns and villages and heading to the desert to preach a harsh repentance, fasting, and penance. It was an austere lifestyle.

No matter if Jesus was John's disciple or if he went to the Jordan for a day visit, Jesus did not follow John's lead. He returned to the desert on a needs-only basis. Primarily itinerant, Jesus's mission was to be in villages and towns proclaiming a repentance of mercy, love, and compassion. I am pleased that I follow Jesus.

John in the desert is a central figure during the season of Advent. We need, however, to be cautious about the desert, and all that it represents, and to approach it carefully and knowingly.

LITURGY AND SACRAMENTS

Ascetical practices in the spiritual life are only ever a means to an end. They are never ends in themselves. Once we lose sight of their purpose, we can get lost in the desert of our penance, which can be a very dangerous place to be.

Some people in the Church these days think our theology and spiritual practices have become too soft and woolly. In some regards, they may have a point, but these "commando" Christians may be following John the Baptist more than Jesus Christ. Truly living a life of mercy, love, and compassion should hold enough tough love with which to be getting on.

Penitential acts do not change God. God is unchanging. They change us so that we might, in turn, change our world for the better so that it reflects the kingdom of God.

Even though we have the ancient and venerable Christian witness of the desert fathers and mothers, St. Anthony was very careful about the centrality of moderation, joy, and compassion that should mark the Christian life in an actual or figurative desert. The story is told about a monk who went to Abba Poemen (ca. 340–450) and asked him, "When we see brothers who are falling asleep during the services, should we arouse them so that they will be watchful?" Poemen said, "For my part, when I see a brother falling asleep, I place his head on my knees and let him rest."

St. Ignatius of Loyola was a man who knew how the most venerable ascetical practices can quickly trip over into self-abasement. Some of this greatest spiritual wisdom was borne out of bitter personal experiences where, in the cave at Manresa in 1522, his penances became so compulsive and obsessive that they did not lead him to

God but were dangerous symptoms of self-destruction. Consequently, St. Ignatius legislated for Jesuits, and advised his religious and lay directees, that we should never undertake any penance, fasting, or extra prayer without the express permission of our confessor or spiritual director.

In and through our preparations in Advent we need to stay focused on what it is that we are seeking: to enable the Lord of life to be reborn in us this Christmas, and that our public lives will mirror the growing freedom of our private prayer. Sometimes for the love and joy of Christmas to flow and flower within us we confront the blocks that get in the road of us living the life of grace.

Taking wise advice, we may need to head to our figurative desert during Advent and spend some time with John the Baptist. But our time there should be marked by us encountering God's mercy and compassion and an assurance of his personal love for us. It should also see us reinvigorated to be sent back from the desert to live and proclaim God's kingdom wherever and however we are.

16

THE JOY OF THE GOSPEL

Over the first millennium of Christianity, Advent was like a late Lent. Both were five weeks long, marked by fasting and penance, and both gave the faithful a day off halfway through.

In Lent, Laetare Sunday is still, roughly, halfway through the five-week season. Advent, however, got shortened to four weeks in the tenth century, and Pope St. Gregory the Great eased the fasting and penitential aspects of this season in the twelfth century, but the now not-so-half-way Gaudete Sunday has remained with us. It is, literally, the "rejoicing Sunday" when we look more directly at the coming of Jesus at Christmas.

All Christians should take joy very seriously. We all know that the Gospels never record Jesus as laughing, but as James Martin, SJ, capably demonstrates in his book *Between Heaven and Mirth: Why Joy, Humor, and Laughter Are at the Heart of the Spiritual Life*, some of the parables in their cultural context would have been hilarious. This can be lost on us.

I have one piece of advice during Advent. If you are a happy Christian, can you please tell your face about it sometime soon. Catholics, especially, can be the gloomiest lot you ever want to see. In my parish at North Sydney, if the commentator has not welcomed people before Mass begins and encouraged the congregation to do likewise around them, then I do it. Usually, the front half of the church warmly indulges me. The back half can look at me contemptuously with a glare that says, "I don't do that crap, get on with it. You have forty-five minutes until I'm out of here."

In Australia, as elsewhere, we have seen some fine young Catholics drift to evangelical churches. While the reasons for this drift are many and varied, every time I have been to a Pentecostal community, I have been generously and explicitly made welcome. The congregation seemed to be genuinely joyful to be there. I always compare that experience with what I see and encounter in some of our own churches.

While some argue that more informal greetings can turn the liturgy into a circus, distract them from their private prayer, and reduce the sacred rites to a "love-in," I never find slippery slope arguments and appeals to an exaggerated emphasis on personal piety at public worship all that convincing.

In fact, our lack of joy can be a symptom of serious spiritual illnesses. It can sometimes show how a believer thinks they need to earn God's salvation, or that they have to save the world, or or that can never be worthy of God's mercy and love. None of these are laughing matters. They are heresies. Only God saves us through unmerited grace. Though we cooperate in salvation, it is the Trinity who effects the salvation of the world. And there is not a person who is beyond the mercy and love of God.

The joy I am advocating here is not walking around with a supercilious smile on one's face, pretending that we do not have a care in the world. That's a pathology. Christian joy is about knowing where we have come from, why we are here, and where we are going. That should put a spring in our step.

Pope Francis has certainly put a spring in my step since becoming pope, and not just because he is a Jesuit. One of the strongest and most distinctive themes in his preaching and teaching so far has been the centrality of joy, culminating in his first apostolic exhortation, "The Joy of the Gospel" (*Evangelii Gaudium*). In a homily at a Mass in the Santa Marta residence chapel one Friday morning, he said,

> A Christian is a man and a woman of joy. Jesus teaches us this, the Church teaches us this.... What is this joy? Is it having fun? No: it is not the same. Fun is good, eh? Having fun is good. But joy is more, it is something else. It is something that does not come from short term economic reasons, from momentary reasons: it is something deeper. It is a gift. Fun, if we want to have fun all the time, in the end becomes shallow, superficial, and also leads us to that state where we lack Christian wisdom, it makes us a little bit stupid, naive, no? Everything is fun... no? Joy is another thing. Joy is a gift from God. It fills us from within. It is like an anointing

of the Spirit. And this joy is the certainty that Jesus is with us and with the Father.[2]

On another occasion the pope said that "if we keep this joy to ourselves it will make us sick in the end, our hearts will grow old and wrinkled and our faces will no longer transmit that great joy—only nostalgia and melancholy, which is not healthy. Sometimes these melancholy Christian faces have more in common with pickled peppers than the joy of having a beautiful life."[3]

Gaudete Sunday is a ritual moment to work against anything that might see us end up as pickled peppers!

---

2. Pope Francis, Homily, "Mass in the Santa Marta residence chapel was concelebrated by the Archbishop of Mérida, Baltazar Enrique Porras Cardozo, and the abbot primate of the Benedictine monks Notker Wolf," May 10, 2013, http://www.archivioradiovaticana.va/storico/2013/05/10/pope_at_mass_christian_joy_far_from_simple_fun_/en1-690760.

3. Pope Francis, Homily, May 10, 2013.

17

THE BABE OF BETHLEHEM

Putting COVID-19 aside, Christmas remains big business in parishes. It's the feast day where people come in droves to the Church, often for their annual visit. It breaks our hearts that they don't turn up each week or that they rarely return for the Easter Triduum, which remains the most important feast in the Church's year. Not even the often well-attended Good Friday service attracts the crowds of Christmas.

It doesn't help that some grumpy clergy begin Christmas Mass by berating the congregation for turning up. Rather than stinging the consciences of the infrequent attenders into action, it appears this rebuke provides further evidence as to why they won't and don't attend at other times.

There has been much talk about Mass numbers in recent years. The pandemic decimated some parishes, and some of the faithful have not returned. Our older people sometimes found an online Mass that gave them convenience and comfort, and they found a new way to pray. Clearly, this is no substitute for gathering with the worshiping community for Eucharist, and even though there is no age limit in our canonical obligation to attend Mass, I know many people who, understandably, have dispensed themselves because of illness, age, or physical frailty. Some still fear getting COVID-19. These days, Catholics are not moved by the threats of eternal damnation for the mortal sin of their nonattendance. In any case, it's always better to be drawn by love than driven by fear.

However, it is a mistake to blame the general slump in church attendance simply on COVID-19 and the lockdowns. That downward spiral has been happening for decades.

The reasons for this drift are many and various. The rise in individualism, the all-out attack of the new atheists, and the criminality uncovered by the sexual abuse crisis have played their parts, but it must be admitted, many of our fellow Catholics have not had an encounter of faith that would lead to a personal relationship with Jesus Christ. They no longer find among us a sense of identity and belonging to draw them back each week, and, while many of them like Jesus and his teaching, they live highly ethical lives without any direct reference to Christianity. If recent surveys are to be believed, most Christians consider an afterlife a remote possibility at best. This makes for a not-so-happy Christmas for us.

We need to be careful of the numbers game. I know of a priest who refuses to go to the Catholic school next door to his parish church "because the students, parents, and teachers do not go to Mass anymore." In this scenario, a person needs to walk the talk before the pastor of souls will have anything to do with you. The spiritual journey has to be on his terms or not at all. Not much missionary imagination or zeal in that approach!

However, the Church has labored in places for centuries that have not led to "bums on seats" and rightly so. Playing the long game, our Catholic community has provided education, health care, and social services to nations for generations that have not led to any major flowering of the local Church. Japan is one such place.

In the 1540s, St. Francis Xavier and his early Jesuit brothers were followed by Franciscans and Dominicans who labored long and hard in the land of the rising sun, until Christianity was banned altogether in 1614. Japan reopened to Christianity in 1853, and ever since, every denomination has sent its best and brightest to serve that great country. Today, as just one example, the Catholic Church runs 831 educational institutions and Japan has given the universal Church 635 saints—almost all of them martyrs. With a population of 125.7 million, only 1.5 percent of them are Christian, and recently Catholics numbered 431,100. If "bums on seats" is the only or main reason for our missionary endeavors, then Japan has been an abject failure, and we should cut and run. But that is not what we have done nor will do.

Christianity's brilliance is not just to play the long game, but to understand our role as leaven in the cultural bread. Our best missionary instinct is to do what the old prayer says (and not written by St. Ignatius of Loyola):

To give and not to count the cost,
to fight and not to heed the wounds,

to toil and not to seek for rest,
to labor and not to ask for reward,
save that of knowing that I do your holy will.

While we all long for the Christmas crowds to turn up throughout the year too, let's start this Christmas by being welcoming, hospitable, joyful, affirming, inclusive, and compassionate, not because it's trendy or a strategy, but because it's what we believe God has done for us in the babe of Bethlehem.

18

PERFECT LOVE

At the risk of wrecking your Christmas, we need to clear up a few things.

I know all our carols and cards say that Jesus was born in December; in a snow-covered stable; was wrapped in swaddling clothes; lay in the manger with the animals; that a star stood vigil; and was later visited by three kings, whose names were Balthazar, Caspar, and Melchior.

But the Gospels don't say any of this—nothing even remotely close to it. It could have snowed on the first Christmas, but the Scriptures don't say that it did. No animals are mentioned. The star in the north did not stand still in the night sky, because stars just don't behave like that, and Jesus probably wasn't even born in December.

In 350, after the Christian community had given the pagan Roman calendar the thorough makeover it richly deserved, Pope Julius I declared that Christmas was to be celebrated on December 25. Rather neatly, the pagan feast of the "birthday of the unconquered Sun" became the "birthday of the all-conquering Son"—the birthday of Jesus, our Lord.

The worst Christmas I ever celebrated was in Manger Square in Bethlehem. I had been looking forward to it. Surely, I hoped, this would be my best Christmas experience. However, by the time I had finally negotiated the traffic jams, the eight security checks, the guards on patrol, and joined the thousands who had been packed into the church, the adventure had lost some of its appeal.

In all the accounts of Christmas we have in the New Testament, we hear the angel begin her announcement of Jesus's birth with the words, "Be not afraid." Given world events over recent months, this greeting is just what we need to hear at Christmas: "Be not afraid."

Fear is a terrible feeling. It cripples us into passivity. It ruins our memories of past or present events, and it undermines dignified, trusting, and respectful relationships. There is an important difference between being vigilant and being frightened, but since the 9/11 terrorist attacks, this difference has become blurred. We have seen people become anxious, change their lifestyle and travel plans, and worry for their future and for that of their children. In a sense, the terrorists win when we change our lives for fear of them.

But we don't need to look to international terror to explain the nature of our fear. Broadly speaking, we fear four things: God, nature, other people, or something within ourselves. It is usually a combination of these things; for some of us, tragically, it is all of them. But to whatever degree fear has come to rule our lives, we need to hear again God's greeting at Christmas: "Be not afraid."

LITURGY AND SACRAMENTS

St. Paul tells us that love drives out all fear. That's what—and who—we celebrate at Christmas: perfect love took human form in Jesus Christ, the Lord. Throughout this joyful season, we celebrate the one whose life, death, and resurrection showed us the way out of our fears; revealed the truth that sets us free; and gave us the life that we can live to the full in this world, and the next.

Christmas is the feast day when God calls us to be as active as possible in bringing God's kingdom to bear in our world.

Christmas is the time when our memories are joined to God's, who has remembered us in our fear.

Christmas is the season when all Christian relationships are defined by the dignity, trust, and respect they bestow on us and on those to whom we relate.

As a result of the babe of Bethlehem, God has shown us that fear is not our calling, and that the saving love of Jesus impels us to take risks in how we live out our faith, hope, and love.

On any day, then, throughout the year, when we face down our fears and live our Christian life to the full, we will discover that Christmas is a moveable feast.

My favorite Advent poem is from John Bell of the Iona Community in Scotland:

Light looked down and saw the darkness.
"I will go there," said light.
Peace looked down and saw war.
"I will go there," said peace.
Love looked down and saw hatred.
"I will go there," said love.

72

So he,
the Lord of Light,
the Prince of Peace,
the King of Love,
came down and crept in beside us. (Rev. John
   Bell of the Iona Community, *Cloth for the
   Cradle*)

No fanfare. No palace. No earthly prince. Christmas celebrates that God crept in beside us. And as a result, there is no part of our lives he will not enter with mercy and love. So, let's invite in again the Lord of Light, the Prince of Peace, the King of Love and live as boldly as we can.

19

THE HOLY FAMILY

From Christmas to the Feast of the Epiphany, our focus understandably turns to the Holy Family. I don't know about your family, but among my clan no one is a canonized saint, immaculately conceived, or the Son of God. The Holy Family is a tough act to follow. We are, however, told to imitate them in "bonds of love." I tried that once—with mixed results.

My family is not demonstrative. We don't have those "love you darling" signoffs at the end of every phone call. A firm handshake for the men and a peck on the cheek for the women is as good as it gets.

During my final high school retreat, I was challenged to "never leave this world not having told the people that you love that you love them." At seventeen, I had never told my mother, brother, or sister that I loved them, and they had never said it to me either. My father died when I was two, so I came back from my school retreat on a mission.

My sister was then working with Mother Teresa in Calcutta, and my brother was working interstate. I sat down and wrote them letters telling them that I loved them. I never heard back—from either of them!

That left my mother. I stayed in one Saturday night, and after dinner, I was in my bedroom. I was so nervous about what I was about to do that you would swear that I was going to ask my mother to marry me. I approached the lounge room where Mom was watching the 7:00 p.m. news. I blurted out, "Mom, I have something very important to tell you."

My mother, not taking her eyes from the screen, casually said, "Oh, yes, what's that?"

"No," I responded, "I've never told you this before, and it's very important that I tell you tonight."

My mother turned off the TV and slowly faced toward me. Now I could tell there were two hearts pumping and two tummies churning in that room. Decades later, my mother told me that she was saying to herself, "Whatever he says next, keep calm, keep calm, keep calm."

I plucked up all my courage and came straight out with it. "Mom, I just want to tell you that I love you." Mom thought that this was the warm act for the big news yet to come.

"Is that it?"

"Yes. Before I die, I wanted to be able to say that I had told you that I love you."

"You're not terminally ill, are you?"

"No, I hope to die an old man, but before then I wanted to tell you that I love you."

Such was her relief she said, "Goodness me, I hope so," and promptly turned the television on again.

As I walked back to my bedroom, I said aloud, "I don't think it was supposed to go like that." There were no violins playing, no warm embraces or statements like,

"At least one of you three ingrates has turned up to tell me that you love me."

What did happen was that my brother and my sister wrote to my mother, "We've had these very weird letters from him."

"Oh, bully for you," my mother replied, "I've had the whole episode in person. But don't worry, it's a phase he's going through."

Hopefully, it is a phase I will never get over, because I am baptized.

One of the problems, today, is that we have devalued the currency of the word *love*. We say we love our car, our house, and ice cream, but we can't truly love *things* because they cannot love us back.

So, if we are going to imitate the bonds of love of the Holy Family, let's start by telling the people that we really do love that we love them. How do we work out who they are? Ask one question: For whom would you die? In my experience that shortens the "I love you" list considerably, and if your dog or cat is seriously on that list, you need therapy immediately. Not that we cannot enjoy our pets, but if we would die for them, then our priorities need reordering.

The Christmas story is all about us being welcomed into the family of God—without exception—and knowing that Jesus came, lived, and died that we might find the way out of the cycle of destruction and death in which humanity had become entrapped; that we might be saved.

Christ didn't leave this world not having told the people whom he loved that he loved us, and, by belonging to his family and following his example in word and deed, nor should we.

20

LIVING IN WONDER OR FEAR

When we go to the cinema, we need to suspend our critical sensibilities to experience the full power of the story. A similar concession is necessary to reap the full benefit of the story of the first Epiphany. Have you ever wondered, for example, why the wise men, who have been guided from the east to Jerusalem, stop there and ask directions from Herod? Surely the star could have kept doing its job and taken them all the way to Bethlehem. And why didn't Herod follow the wise men, or at least send a spy behind them, rather than ask them to send word back to him when they had found him? Furthermore, whatever happened to these wise guys? They are the first in Matthew's Gospel to recognize who Jesus is, and yet they vanish from Jesus's life as quickly as they came into it.

Like many screenwriters, Matthew plays with history for another purpose. Like cinemagoers, we're happy to suspend our questions and look beyond the story's details so we can enjoy the profound picture that is being painted for us. And profound it is. These dreaming star-gazers in Matthew's Gospel point to the radical nature of the kingdom revealed in Jesus Christ. This story takes on an even more radical tone when we remember that Matthew is writing for a predominantly Jewish community. The people of Israel considered themselves to be the chosen people, and they hoped and longed to see the Messiah who God had promised to them. Yet here are three Gentiles—in other words, not among those to whom the promise had been made—who are among the first to see and believe in Jesus.

Throughout his Gospel, Matthew is at pains to show how the Jews missed out on recognizing Jesus because they were locked in their fears. King Herod is the first public official to be portrayed in such a way, but he is by no means the last or the least. Pilate is the bookend to Herod, showing a similar blindness. Matthew links these two rulers. Their fear of the threat posed by Jesus, who he is and how he lives, leads in each case to death—Herod's slaughter of the innocents and Pilate's murder of Jesus.

Matthew's story is a wonderful interplay between wonder and fear. We're told only five things about the wise men from the east: they follow the rising star; they ask directions in a foreign land; they're overwhelmed with joy at finding the child at Bethlehem; they're warned in a dream about Herod; and they go home by another road. This last observation is a delicious detail. One path, the familiar route, the way they knew, would have led to death; instead, they trusted their dreams and took a different path. It led to life. Unlike the wise men,

Herod is frightened at the prospect of a pretender to his throne. He whips up fear in Jerusalem and tries to trick the Magi into telling him where he can find the child. But his deceit is uncovered, and he is left without knowledge. His fears spiral.

In twelve verses, Matthew paints a portrait of wonder. If we are wise followers of the babe of Bethlehem, we need to be shrewd in dealing with power; to keep our eyes on the journey that will bring joy and fulfillment as well as suffering; to believe in dreams; to pray that we will never be so sure of how God works in our world that we miss seeing the very thing we long to behold; and to be prepared to change course so that we can always choose life.

Matthew also tells us that the enemy of the Christian life is fear. So often, our reaction to Jesus can be like Herod's. We can feel threatened and frightened. We want to silence the voices that call us to live out the reign of God and listen instead to those who whisper of the costs involved. Fear entraps us and infects those around us. We are often most fearful when we risk losing power and control, so we lie, become deceitful, and cheat to maintain our position at all costs. As with Herod and Pilate, that way ends in death.

So, this story is far more than a travel log of exotic Persian kings. It's the story of the choices that lie before all who want to worship Jesus. Once again, at the dawn of each New Year, the choice is ours: Do we want to live in wonder or in fear?

PART THREE

SOCIETY

21

PUBLIC VERSUS PRIVATE

One of the greatest tensions in modern society is the one between the public and the private spheres. It's hard to know where one domain stops and the other starts. Social media has been the disruptor in this space, enabling people to post, share, and tag extraordinary details of their hitherto private lives with billions of people globally. Many of these postings are harmless or banal, but some have far-reaching outcomes that could never have been foreseen at the time. Some of us have been lulled into a false sense of privacy. It's called *social* media for a reason.

Personally, I work on the assumption that anything I email, share, like, or post online might be shared with the rest of the world at some stage. I am also of the opinion that some people are so busy posting their experiences online that they are not actually having any. The online world is an encouragement to move on from important events happening in the real world far too quickly, without taking the time to deepen the experience. This is what Adolfo Nicolás, SJ, the former Superior General of the Jesuit order, was warning us against, when he said that social media is "the globalization of superficiality." It is the very opposite of the approach of St. Ignatius of Loyola, who urged us to savor experience and learn from it, to enjoy it, and when appropriate, to repent of it, so that we might make better decisions.

Boris Johnson and Israel Folau make unlikely twins in the tense space between public and private. Folau, the fundamentalist Christian rugby player, did not foresee the outcome of posting a meme of 1 Corinthians 6:9–10 on his Instagram account with this stark admonition: "WARNING Drunks, Homosexuals, Adulterers, Liars, Fornicators, Thieves, Atheists, Idolaters HELL AWAITS YOU, REPENT! ONLY JESUS SAVES [sic]." Days later, he was sacked from the Australian rugby team. He launched legal proceedings against Rugby Australia, saying, "No Australian of any faith should be fired for practicing their religion."

It's worth noting that, to have read Mr. Folau's post, you had to have signed on to be one of his Instagram followers. He had a history of posting Bible quotes and harsh condemnations, and so those who followed him on social media would have already known his views. Where do private/public obligations start and end? You get what you follow! Folau is entitled to his opinions; I am entitled to reject them. We have been conned into believing that each opinion is of equal value. I believe Folau abuses Scripture for his own end; until he gets to a tattoo removalist, a literal reading of Leviticus 19 would mean that he is going to hell along with those he wants to save. His legal case will come down to his private contractual obligations regarding his very highly paid public profile as an employee of Rugby Australia.

The case of Boris Johnson is a very different private/public matter. The neighbors of Johnson's partner recorded the couple having a row and reported it to the police, who spoke to all occupants of Johnson's address, who were safe and well. The recording was passed to a daily newspaper, which released transcripts of the exchanges. To what degree do we have a right to know about the private lives of our elected public officials, especially those who aspire to be prime minister?

In Psalm 130, the Psalmist says, "If you, O LORD, should mark iniquities, Lord, who could stand?" Indeed. However, this verse needs to be read beside other texts in relation to things done in the dark being exposed to the light. Some argue that we only have a right to know the details of someone's private behavior insofar as it affects public decision-making. Many previous generations would have been outraged if they knew what we know about their king, queen, president, prime minister, or pope. While there are different types of privacy—a person's feelings; their "space"; what individuals have said and written, perhaps in the distant past; their family and personal history—through it all, we are what we do. My public self is intimately connected to my private self. While everyone is entitled to a private space, if we artificially break the link between public and private, then democracies are electing actors, people who seek our approval to perform on the public stage, but who insist on having another personality and life history in a hermetically sealed space out of public view.

It is a subtle distinction and a matter of degree; the private/public space is changing quickly. With the increasing dominance of personality politics, the public's legitimate "right to know" is in danger of becoming confused with our insatiable tabloid desire to know as much as we can about every public figure. A revered American basketball coach once said, "The true test of a man's character is what he does when no one is watching."[1] I agree. And while respecting truly private spaces, I would hope that those who are richly rewarded for their public roles are people of character when also out of the media spotlight.

---

1. John Wooden, cited by Walter Pavlo, "Character Is What You Do When EVERYONE Is Watching," *Forbes*, October 23, 2012, https://www.forbes.com/sites/walterpavlo/2012/10/23/character-is-what-you-do-when-everyone-is-watching/?sh=4a9d6f77fc6d.

22

GOD'S MERCY AND LOVE

Immediately before I read *Christ Is Alive*, Pope Francis's post-synodal apostolic exhortation on young people, I had plowed through the 2019 Australian government report *The Mental Health of Children and Adolescents*. That document, alerting us to the deteriorating mental health of young Australians, makes grim reading. We are not alone in experiencing this problem. Something is terribly wrong when in most developed countries the biggest killer of young adults is now suicide.

Rightly and understandably, the tone of *Christ Is Alive* is much more upbeat, but one word ties these two documents together: *meaning*, or the lack of it. The government report talks constantly about "meaninglessness" as one of the main drivers for poor mental health. Pope Francis mentions the word *meaning* forty times.

In the government study, *meaninglessness* is defined as when a person feels they do not matter in the scheme of things, not to any other person, and not to the community. The increase in meaninglessness is connected to a rise in utilitarianism, individualism, and to personal autonomy being recognized as an absolute value: my worth or meaning is gauged by money and status: "I am what I do"; "No one can tell me what to do, especially with my body." The study goes on to list several causes, a few of which have been around for a while: marriage breakdown; extended families and local communities that fail to make young people feel connected and instead feeling they belong to no one; "helicopter parents" leaving their children feeling anxious and smothered; having so many choices that they are immobilized; and being inculcated in the attitude that "I can achieve anything I want," leading to unrealistic expectations and lack of awareness of the preparation and hard work that is needed to achieve a goal.

Social media comes under careful and critical analysis in both the government's report and in the papal document. The government report highlights the seeming contradiction between never having more possibilities for making connections online, and at the same time young adults never feeling more isolated. In the online world, "friends," whom one may never have met, are considered real friends; "likes," or the lack of them, control self-esteem and mood; and the fallout from addictions, including to online pornography, is devastating.

The government's mental health report argues for further study, new protocols, and improved procedures. These are worthwhile and important and will hopefully have an impact. However, Pope Francis's suggested approach gets closer to the roots of the problem by talking about hope. He mentions it forty-one times;

the government document never mentions it once. Yet meaninglessness is born of hopelessness.

Francis links hope to encouragement, to pursuing dreams, to joy, to being forgiven and having compassion, to seeking the truth, to forming consciences, and being mentored and accompanied here on earth and by the cloud of witnesses in heaven. And he argues against

> those who worship the "goddess of lament."...
> She is a false goddess: she makes you take the wrong road. When everything seems to be standing still and stagnant, when our personal issues trouble us, and social problems do not meet with the right responses, it does no good to give up. Jesus is the way: welcome him into your "boat" and put out into the deep! He is the Lord! He changes the way we see life. Faith in Jesus leads to greater hope, to a certainty based not on our qualities and skills, but on the word of God, on the invitation that comes from him. Without making too many human calculations, and without worrying about things that challenge your security, put out into the deep.[2]

In my many dealings with young people, most poignantly at the funerals of their friends who have taken their own lives, they respond most to a hope that trusts in God's mercy and love, that knows that we are connected to a greater story, to a welcoming and inclusive Catholic community, and to looking for a life yet to come. Christian hope affirms and celebrates that we know

---

2. Pope Francis, "Ecumenical and Interreligious Meeting with Young People," Pastoral Centre (Skopje), May 7, 2019, www.vatican.va.

where we have come from, why we are here, and where we are going, and that we are not doing this on our own.

A government report can never say it, but the breakdown in communities of hope, especially the breakdown in faith communities of the kind that we are experiencing in the Church, has had negative effects on the mental well-being not just of young Catholics but of young people in the wider community. While shouldering our fair share of the blame for our faith not attracting young people in anything like the way we would like to see— partly because our community of hope is often seen by young people as hopeless—those of us who know that Christ is alive have to redouble our efforts to live our Christian faith with hope and joy. The mental health of our children depends on it.

23

IN GOD WE TRUST

In recent decades, the Vatican has condemned the books of several theologians and writers from the United States. Whatever the arguments for these measures in individual cases, I have never been able to reconcile the portrait of the U.S. Catholic Church as radical or maverick with my experience of its parish life. As a native Australian who has visited, studied, and worked off and on in the United States for many years, I am always struck by the difference between the views of some high-profile Catholic academics and the reality in the pews.

I often work in the United States, speaking in parishes and at conferences and presiding at the Eucharist for a variety of groups in many settings. In my experience, the Church there is one of the most faithful Catholic communities in the world.

Though the numbers there are down from the old high-water mark, the Mass attendance rate is still among the highest of any developed country in the world. The ethnic and social diversity is as rich as is the age range, and parishes, by and large, have not lost parents with young families.

Reflecting the wider culture, Catholics in the United States tend to be enthusiastic and generous. And because money is allocated to paying for liturgy directors and well-trained musicians, the Sunday Mass is often celebrated with reverence and joy—and with the full, active, and conscious participation of the people. The congregations even want to like the homilist and are generous in their response.

Moreover, for all the incessant criticism from some U.S. Catholic commentators that Pope Francis is confusing the faithful, every time I mention the pope and his leadership of the Church, there is affectionate acclamation.

Nevertheless, there are some tensions and contradictions in U.S. Catholicism that still unnerve me. I am never comfortable when I see national flags of any country, including the Holy See, present in the sanctuary. The weekly prayers for the men and women serving in the defense force always brings me up short, not because we should not pray for them—of course we should—but because we need to be careful that our prayers do not inhibit us from critically engaging with every conflict upon which our nation engages.

Cardinal Robert Sarah would be pleased to see the number of people who choose to receive communion on the tongue, which is their right; but I was surprised when presiding at a Catholic grade school Mass that around one-third of the children received it this way. The number of Catholic children who are now home schooled is said to be at an all-time high. This makes me nervous; I have met too many adults who have told me they regret their parents' decision not to allow them to attend school.

Before or during almost every Mass I attend, there is a pro-life prayer. These express valuable statements of our faith, though they sometimes lack pastoral sensitivity. While we defend the rights of the unborn, we should be reaching out in mercy and compassion to the women sitting in the congregation who have been through an abortion. It is not either/or. It is both/and.

I was touched by the public and civic honors bestowed on Billy Graham after his death by a grateful nation. However, the proud and public religiosity of this great country only adds to the deep obligations that following Christ demands regarding the poor, the vulnerable, refugees, and the uninsured.

I was in Florida during a tragic high school shooting. I have never once heard a bishop or any other Catholic figure participate in the endless cable news debates about gun control, which must also be a right-to-life issue. When I ask about gun control at the "coffee and donuts" that follows almost every Sunday parish Mass, I am always shocked at how more than a few good and faithful Catholics argue strongly for the right to bear arms. A week ago, I was shown a gun that a parishioner had brought with him to Mass. I did not feel safer.

The constant wrangling over gun control has helped me see the underlying violence that permeates the United States; it's present everywhere in the world, but it seems closer to the surface there because of the gregarious way North Americans explore their feelings and issues in public. And it has helped me to understand the violent tone that characterizes many Catholic bloggers there. Their camera and their keyboard are their weapons of choice.

SOCIETY

Their brutal character assassinations and wild and bitter assaults on those whom they perceive to be the enemies of the truth are inexcusably ugly and uncharitable.

I love the United States, and I love U.S. Catholics—but I am pleased that for all of us it is in God we have to trust.

24

HAPPINESS VERSUS JOY

Happiness has become an industry that is selling us a lie.

Barry Larkin committed suicide in 1995. None of his family or friends knew that he was chronically depressed. His son, Gavin, was so shocked by his much-loved father's death that it eventually led him to cofound the R U OK? movement. Each year, on the second Thursday in September, Australians are encouraged to contact someone they know who might be going through a difficult patch and ask, "Are you OK?" The simplicity of the challenge combined with the complexity of our contemporary mental health culture has struck a chord. R U OK? has taken off, and not just on one day of the year.

Last year, as the promotion for the campaign ramped up, I called two friends, both aged under thirty, whom I knew were struggling, one with a bitter divorce, the other with ill health. The friend battling cancer was in better spirits and had good family support. Within seconds of asking my friend going through a difficult divorce if he was OK, he burst into tears and sobbed. Only the thought of leaving his children fatherless was stopping him from ending his life. Though it wasn't a bad start, my friend needed more than a phone call. He needed a lot of help.

It is a shocking reality that, in the developed world, the greatest cause of death of young people under thirty is not the abuse of drugs or alcohol or misadventure, but suicide. Young adults living in the countries with the highest standards of living and with the greatest educational opportunities should, in theory, have the most to live for. Yet in a generation that is sometimes described as the most socially connected ever, the feeling of isolation appears to be pandemic. Many contemporary young people are *not* OK.

The reasons for this poor state of mental health, the increase in suicide (or "self-delivery," as suicide is now sometimes called) and attempted suicide, are many and complex, but, as Hugh Mackay argues in *The Good Life*, happiness has become an industry that is selling all of us a lie. "I don't mind people being happy—but the idea that everything we do is part of the pursuit of happiness seems to me a really dangerous idea and has led to a contemporary disease in Western society, which is fear of sadness," Mackay writes. "We're kind of teaching our kids that happiness is the default position—it's rubbish. Wholeness is what we ought to be striving for and part of that is sadness, disappointment, frustration, failure; all of those things which make us who we are....I'd like just for a year to have a moratorium on the word 'happiness' and to replace it with the word 'wholeness.'"[3]

Mackay is not on his own. I have lost count of the number of parents who say to me, "I don't care what my kids do, as long as they're happy." Although it may be just a casual throwaway line, it is a symptom of a deeper anxiety. Why are we setting our children up for such failure? Why don't Christian parents say, "I want my children to be faithful, hopeful, loving, just, and good"? Living those virtues will not always lead to happiness, but it will bring something more valuable and precious: joy.

Joy is one the great themes in the teaching of Pope Francis. Christian joy is not the same as happiness. Christian joy celebrates that we know where we have come from, why we are here, and where we are going. It moves away from trying to find the easy side of living and to confront the inevitable tough moments in our lives, and to embrace suffering as an inescapable reality in the human condition. It seeks to be resilient in the face of adversity by embodying Jesus's call to love God and our neighbor as we love ourselves. And it tells us that we are not meant to live isolated lives as "rocks and islands," as the song by Simon and Garfunkel informs us. There was a good reason why Jesus sent the disciples out in twos.

Gavin Larkin's wife, Maryanne, found out how tragic and unhappy life can truly be. Gavin died in 2011 of lymphoma at the age of forty-two, sixteen years after his father's suicide. Their son, Gus, died in 2013 from brain cancer at the age of fifteen. I hope people call Maryanne

3. Hugh Mackay, *The Good Life: What Makes a Life Worth Living?* (Sydney: Macmillan, 2013).

to ask her if she is OK. We need to do the same for someone we know who may be struggling, especially if he or she is young, because so many young people have been sold a lie, and now that life is not as happy as they were promised it would be, some find they have no hope for the future. Living Christian joy is not easy nor straightforward, but setting out on this path might be the way to be more than OK.

25

RELIGIOUS LIBERTY

I've never wanted to see habited and veiled Catholic nuns more in my life. At French beaches. In droves.

Although the battle of the burkini can be read in a variety of ways, it is but the most recent assault on religious freedom.

Religious liberty is not about any specific religion; it is about how Western secular pluralistic democracies enshrine the rights of their citizens to the free exercise of religion and, rightly, to defend the rights of others to have no religion at all.

Several countries have already banned the wearing of crosses in the workplace. Crucifixes have been ordered to be removed from classrooms not in Islamic republics but in Ireland, Spain, France, the Czech Republic, and Italy.

Holy ground for the dead is not even immune. There are no religious symbols at the 9/11 memorial, which, especially for the families of the victims, is a monumental cemetery. And the city of Dudley, Massachusetts, is off to federal court over their rejection of the local Islamic community wanting to open a dedicated cemetery there.

These events make me wonder about the outcomes of these religiously intolerant movements. For instance, imagine if in nations with Christian heritages we decided to publicly rid ourselves of all our religious baggage. There would be unforeseen consequences.

St. Valentine's Day, for example, named after a third-century Roman martyr who died out of love for Christ, would have to be renamed Cupid's day, except Cupid was also the Greek god of love.

Christmas Day, gifts, trees, carols, cribs, nativity plays, and meals would be banished or, at least, officially rebranded as the secular feast of excess it has already become. Good Friday and Easter would be outlawed as public commemorations. Maybe the more commercially successful Mothers and Fathers Days could easily replace them as secular public holidays.

All references to God on secular coats of arms, money, and in all oaths of allegiance, and vows to tell the truth "so help me God" would have to be dismissed. There could be no swearing on a Bible, ever, and no religious prayers uttered anywhere in the civic arena.

National songs and hymns would need a makeover so that God would no longer be saving the king, defending New Zealand, or making Canada glorious and free. There could be no state memorial services at national cathedrals or abbeys. Presumably, this would be the end of the taxpayer-funded British royal coronations, funerals, and weddings in the Church of England, as they would now become private religious events.

All references directly related to the cross of Christ would have to be changed because the Red Cross and the Victoria Cross, just to name two, owe their origins to the one upon which Jesus died.

Even Hollywood would need to be renamed because, in 1886, it was called that by the devout Methodist, Mrs. H. H. Wilcox, in honor of her devotion to the original holy wood.

Choirs and orchestras that receive any share of government funding would not be allowed to perform any type of religious music. The *Messiah* and most of Bach would be banned.

All religious art, including indigenous religious art and artifacts, would have to be withdrawn from public view or sold to private collectors. Furthermore, public libraries could raise money for the poor by selling off all their religious volumes, starting with their antiquarian Bibles.

No longer would anyone be publicly called a godparent.

Regardless of the good work they do, all religious schools, healthcare institutions, social services, and development agencies would be barred from receiving any state aid.

Sporting groups called the demons, devils, saints, angels, friars, cardinals, or crusaders may need a name change.

Any Christian religious procession, a peal from the belfry, a call to prayer from a minaret, the blast of the shofar, and the ringing of the Buddhist *bonshō* could be outlawed as civil disturbances; in several places they already are.

Finally, phrases with biblical and religious origins might have to be dropped from public discourse, like talking of a "Good Samaritan," a "prodigal son," a "doubting Thomas," or referring to a meal seemingly prepared from nowhere as the "loaves and the fish."

Does all this sound absurd? It could be. I sincerely hope it is, but who gets to pick and choose what is and is not tolerated from this point on?

France is not about a burkini; it is about the religious liberty of all of us in an increasingly hostile secular society.

26

A PAUPER'S FUNERAL

The first funeral I ever did was a week after arriving as a deacon at St. Canice's, Kings Cross, the red-light district of Sydney. I was asked to do a "pauper's funeral," an appalling Dickensian name for a state-funded cremation.

Karl was an alcoholic and homeless man who had died on the street. The two saintly religious sisters who had cared for him for years organized his funeral.

The sisters thought it was unlikely that anyone else would turn up. On the day, there were three other mourners in attendance. After the readings and prayers, and because I had never met Karl, I invited the congregation to share their memories of their deceased friend. Toward the back of the chapel, the sisters shook their heads. It was too late. A short stout woman was on her feet and was next to the coffin. "Thank you very much, Father," she said differentially, and then she let loose. "Karl," she yelled, pointing at the coffin, "you were a bastard. You were a bastard in the morning, a bastard in the evening, and a bastard at nighttime." And this theme, and that word, went on and on. The sisters started crying with laughter and gave me a look that said, "You got yourself into this; get yourself out of it."

After two minutes, I stood up and moved toward the eulogist; she took the cue and said, "So, in conclusion, I'd like to say, Karl, you were a spherical bastard, because anyway we looked at you, you were a bastard." And with that, turned to me and said sweetly, as though she had just delivered a loving tribute, "Thank you so much, Father," and sat down. The sisters were in hysterics.

Esme had been Karl's wife. They had both been lawyers. I knew by her sophisticated use of the word *spherical* that she was an educated woman, but they had both been codependent alcoholics, and they blamed each other for the way their marriage and their adult lives fell apart.

This was quite a way to start my ministry to all souls. I wondered if all my funerals were going to be this action-packed.

Encouraged by the author of 2 Maccabees, All Souls' Day has its roots in the sixth-century Benedictine tradition of praying to the dead. It was a way of recognizing that human bonds go beyond death. By the tenth century, this feast was about praying for the dead, that they might know the merciful love of God. St. Odilo of Cluny fixed this feast on November 2, 998, at his abbey at Cluny. Rome adopted and mandated it in the fourteenth century.

In our increasingly secular society, it's interesting to note that the word *soul* persists in ordinary conversation. Many nonreligious people use this most religious of terms to describe another person. We often hear how others are lonely, distressed, or lost souls. It can be said that someone has a "beautiful soul" or that a piece of music, a painting, or other work of art "stirred my soul." We describe mellow jazz as "soulful" and still alert others to distress by an SOS, "save our souls." These uses of the word reinforce St. Thomas Aquinas's teaching that the soul makes us human and sets us apart from other animals.

Nearly all the great religions of the world believe in a soul, or its equivalent—something that survives the annihilation of the body in death. I have come to the opinion that whatever else might characterize the soul, memory is integral to it. For example, the funerals of Alzheimer sufferers are rarely sad occasions because the family invariably says that they "lost" their loved one months or years before because he or she couldn't remember anyone or anything.

Memory as a constitutive element in my soul means that when I meet God face-to-face, I will remember who I am and how I lived, and God will remember me. It's also a comfort for us to think that we will be reunited with those we have loved who have died before us, because we will remember each other.

And what's best about a "remembering soul" is that it is purified. If we think of purgatory as a stage rather than a place, then it's possible to reclaim it as a moment where our memory is purified so that we can be at peace with God for eternity.

So, as we remember our "departed souls," let's never forget God's saving love, live lives worthy of it here and now, and become the person who, at our funeral, might be termed a spherical saint.

27

CONFRONTING RIGIDITY

These days, buzzwords and taglines in marketing are everything: short, immediate disclosures that pique interest or point to a larger message. Whether it's intentional or not, Pope Francis is a master of this communication.

When people—both inside and outside the Church—think about Francis, words like *mercy, joy, compassion, care for the environment, a Church of the poor for the poor*, and possibly even *reform* immediately come to mind.

In recent weeks, however, it struck me that there is another buzzword that he mentions just as much as these others: *rigidity*. Google "pope francis rigidity" and you will discover that this theme is an overarching narrative of this pontificate and possibly one of the least explored.

When Francis addresses this topic, it's with passion. In no uncertain terms he has told bishops, priests, seminarians, religious, young Catholics, liturgists, canon lawyers, and ecumenists, among many others, to stop being rigid. While calling the Church to be faithful to the Gospels and the best of our received Catholic tradition, the pope rails against those who interpret, teach, or apply that tradition "with hostile inflexibility."

Confronting rigidity is not necessarily partisan. It attends to ideology. I know people on the liberal and traditional extremes of our Catholic community who are equally rigid. For example, I know priests who cannot wear clerical dress under any circumstances, and others who cannot but wear it. In the context of their lives, custom and appropriateness count for nothing. They are equally unfree.

Often when Pope Francis raises the "illness of rigidity," he also speaks about freedom, and this holds the Ignatian key to his very traditional and Catholic message.

The founder of the Jesuits, St. Ignatius of Loyola, was given to scruples. At one stage, they were so bad that he became emotionally crippled by them. He wrestled against them for the last thirty-four years of his life, and he came to see that one of the great consolations of the Holy Spirit was freedom from rigidity, of being able to "let go and let God." With God's grace, Ignatius could appropriately deal with his ego to the degree that he could rejoice at being a creature and not seek to act as the Creator. He knew interior freedom was one of the manifest signs of the Spirit.

Ignatius was convinced that detachment from anything that stopped us being faithful, hopeful, and loving in our following of Christ was the goal of the spiritual life. This applied corporately as well as personally.

In his First Principle and Foundation of his *Spiritual Exercises*, Ignatius talks about "making use of those things that help to bring us closer to God and leaving aside those things that don't." His famous twice-daily Examen was never meant to be about the scrupulous interrogation it later became, but rather, as we examen our conscience over time, we come to see the patterns that enable us to choose freedom in Christ and deal with those patterns that imprison us in fear.

Just when we might think that Ignatius only applied this to one's personal life or to interior freedom, it is good to know that, when he wrote his elaborate *Constitutions* for the Society of Jesus, he wrote in many injunctions about local flexibility, subjective application, and ultimately following what the Lord may require. St. Ignatius believed in institutional flexibility and freedom because he saw it opened the Church to the promptings of the Holy Spirit. So, when Pope Francis confronts rigidity, he is betraying his Ignatian roots.

The present pope is fascinating because he cannot be classified by the usual sociopolitical categories of liberal/conservative or left/right. He is neither and both and all of them because like the wise master of a house who brings out of his treasure what is new and old, it rests on discerning how to live the authentic gospel of Jesus Christ in the here and now. From bitter experience, St. Ignatius mistrusted one-size-fits-all solutions. So does Pope Francis.

Francis rails against the young and the old in the Church who show no pastoral flexibility because he believes it's a symptom of a spiritual disease that leads to being defensive and hypocritical. "A Catholic should not be afraid of the open sea nor look for shelter in safe havens. The Lord calls us to go out on mission, to go far off, and not retire to safeguard our certainties."

For Francis, like Ignatius, this is personal.

28

COMPASSION VERSUS ACCOUNTABILITY

When the film *Spotlight* opened in many countries, it was one of the angriest films many had ever seen.

In the Bible, we hear about righteous anger, where God or humanity realizes something is so wrong that "holy anger" is the first and right response. In the Scriptures, this anger often leads to justice, to making things right.

Spotlight is an occasion for holy, righteous anger, and every adult Catholic should see it. Not because it is easy watching, but because it is necessary watching. The time to look away has gone.

The first meaning of this film's title refers to the team of award-winning investigative journalists at the *Boston Globe*. In the late 1990s, they become aware of several Catholic priests who had been accused of child sexual abuse. In the early days of their investigation, they unearth evidence that the Catholic Archdiocese of Boston had gone to extraordinary lengths to cover up the activities of these pedophile priests, and silence victims through payoffs, legal threats, and personal intimidation.

The team starts out believing that they are looking at isolated, criminal individuals: the "rotten apple" theory. Within a year, they discover there have been credible or accepted allegations against ninety priests, 6 percent of the total clergy in the archdiocese. Some of these men were moved to various other dioceses in the United States where they raped and abused other children. In 2011, Boston's Cardinal O'Malley made public the full list of offending clergy: a total of 159 men.

By 2001, rumors of the newspaper's investigation emerged. Some powerful men wanted to shut down the investigation. The journalists were personally targeted and harassed. The newspaper and its reporters press on. "They knew and they let it happen! To KIDS! Okay? It could have been you, it could have been me, it could have been any of us. We gotta nail these scumbags! We gotta show people that nobody can get away with this; not a priest, or a cardinal or a freaking pope!"

From June to December 2002, the *Boston Globe* published thirteen lengthy reports about the crimes and their cover-up, culminating in the resignation of Cardinal Law as archbishop of Boston on December 14, 2002. The paper, and its first Jewish editor, came under sustained attack for being "anti-Catholic." In 2003, the *Spotlight* team won the Pulitzer Prize for Journalism for Public Service for their fearless and outstanding work.

The second more obvious meaning of *Spotlight* is the pool of light wherein the watcher's attention is singularly focused upon one place on the stage. In the history theater, depending on what happens in that prolonged, harsh pool of exposure, careers and reputations have been made or destroyed.

This film not only casts its forensic gaze against the Catholic Church and complicit civic institutions regarding child sexual abuse, but also on the *Globe*. Since 1976, victims, their families, and lawyers had been telling the *Boston Globe* about the crimes, the criminals, and the scale of the cover up. The editorial staff could not or would not see what was in front of them.

In Australia, this film was released at a critical time as the Royal Commission into Institutional Responses to Child Sexual Abuse was more than halfway through its investigation. The Commission was clearly informing our community that this shameful and criminal chapter is not "a media beat-up from an anti-Catholic press" or "it's just a few sick individuals." Even though we now know that there has been a pandemic of sexual abuse of minors—in family homes, in every religious group as well as all welfare and government institutions that have had long-lasting dealings with children—this shocking context affords us no comfort or excuse. For as Francis Sullivan, the head of the Church's Truth, Justice and Healing Council recently stated, "As [Church] witness after witness fronts the Royal Commission the pretense falls away....Many have said that this Royal Commission is vitally important for the future of the Catholic Church in Australia. Quite clearly the Church has not been able to be as honest with itself as it has had to be in these hearings. Now the challenge is to explain why this tragic scandal occurred and how it can be prevented from ever happening again."

SOCIETY

So why watch this very tough and demanding film? Because victims and their families deserve it.

May it make us both "as mad as hell" and "not take this anymore," but more importantly, may it enable that holy, righteous anger to demand complete transparency and accountability from every sector of our own community. That might just be the start of bringing God's justice and healing to survivors.

Whether we like it or not, now we are all in the spotlight—and there is nowhere to hide.

29

ORGANIZED RELIGION

In February 2013, the Australian Royal Commission into Institutional Responses to Child Sexual Abuse released data recording the number of cases of abuse since 1950. There has been some dispute about how the numbers were crunched, but however you look at them, the extent of the abuse of children by priests that they reveal is shocking and disturbing.

People outside Australia might not care much about this survey of national opinion except that it is a further snapshot that confirms the declining fortunes of institutional Christianity in the West. From the reaction of the mainstream media in Australia, one could be forgiven for thinking that the recent census had been solely on religious belief or unbelief. The headline that writers delighted in pointing out was how the census showed that organized religion was on the wane, and hopefully, many said, on the way out completely. It was all a little odd. The question regarding religion was just one of sixty on the form, and it was one of only two that were optional—there were 1.9 million of my 24.5 million compatriots who did not answer the question.

The numbers are certainly challenging but do not quite demonstrate the triumph of atheism in Australia that some long for. While 60.3 percent of Australians indicated that they had "some" religion, 30.1 percent indicated they had none, dramatically up from 22.3 percent six years ago. Despite an increase in Pentecostal churches, Christianity decreased to 52.1 percent of the population, while both Hinduism and Islam grew. The Australian Catholic community now constitutes 22.6 percent of the nation, down from 25.3 percent. While this is a significant drop, given the unrelentingly bad news the Church has attracted in recent years—much of it warranted—it is surprising that it had only lost 147,438 adherents. I thought we would have hemorrhaged much more. Not surprisingly, it was those between the ages of 18 and 35 years who no longer find a home among us. The Synod on Young People of 2018 came at the right time and with the right focus.

What is of wider concern is the giddy delight of commentators at the decline of organized religion. Its demise is gleefully welcomed by those who seem to take satisfaction in the humiliation of every institution. We should tread very carefully here. I cannot think of a single traditional social institution that presently enjoys anything like universal affection or support among Australians. We have lurched from uncritical respect to kneejerk cynicism about everything. Politicians are on the nose, the police are on the take, the judiciary is corrupt, lawyers are leeches, civil servants are incompetent, teachers are lazy, journalists are liars, doctors are ripping off the system, sports stars are cheats, priests are pedophiles, and the armed forces lurch from one scandal to the next. It's hard to know who or what we value—if we value anything at all!

These sweeping generalizations and stereotypes could be dismissed as just that if I did not hear them so regularly asserted. The more they go unchallenged, the greater claim they have on the social narrative. I am all for independent inquiries into institutions, for greater accountability, more open access for change and reform—in some cases radical reform—of our institutions. "To live is to change, and to be perfect is to have changed often," as John Henry Newman wisely taught. Every organization needs to adapt to better meet the demands they seek to serve. Maybe some have reached their use-by date, at least in their current form, but I cannot see how the greater good is served by the constant denigration of the institutional glue that binds us together.

At their best, institutions serve the common values to which we all aspire. Although their frameworks, codes, behaviors, roles, structures, customs, and rituals must continually evolve, the wholesale unthinking dismissal of their worth is already having consequences. The best of politics, law and order, the civil service, education, the media, health care, sport, religion, and the defense forces anchor us in shared values, provide cohesion and stability, and promote a sense of belonging. If they go, or if our trust in them collapses, it will create a vacuum, and we might learn the truth of the old saying that, if we stand for nothing, then we could fall for anything.

30

SCANDAL

In 1994, after I had spoken at a conference entitled "Women and Men and the Future of the Church," I received a letter of sharp rebuke from the local bishop.

I had argued that, given the pope had recently ruled out the ordination of women to the priesthood, we should move apace to return women to the order of deacons and to readmit laypeople to the College of Cardinals, including laywomen. The bishop was incensed that I would present such "personal and maverick ideas" in his diocese.

Within a few short years, I found myself in good company, with Cardinal Martini speaking in favor of women cardinals, and, more recently, in even better company, with Pope Francis opening the way to the possibility of women deacons. My ideas have turned out to be less personal and less maverick than the furious bishop realized.

His letter went on: "What is most shocking is that you have committed grave sins for a Catholic priest: confusing the lay faithful; being publicly disloyal to the pope and the College of Bishops; and providing scandal— which can only be the work of the evil one." Heavy stuff!

For the record, the magisterium of the Church has never declared that women cannot be deacons or cardinals, so, despite the bishop's protestations, these were issues for serious debate—and they still are.

The bishop is long dead, but I wonder what he would make of the very public dissent from the teaching of the Synod of Bishops and the pope that was expressed by a small group of cardinals, the petition from forty-five priests and theologians, and the regular social media campaigns being mounted by so-called loyal Catholics against the present magisterium.

I have lost count of how many times I have been told over the years that "the Church is not a democracy." Throughout the pontificates of St. John Paul II and Benedict XVI we were told that fidelity to the pope was a touchstone of orthodoxy, as opposed to what individual Catholics might think or feel. But now that some Catholics strongly disagree with what the present universal pastor says, all bets are off when it comes to garnering and mobilizing support.

How things have changed. For thirty years, the term *cafeteria Catholic* was derisively applied to those who dared dissent from the Catholic line. Now we have discovered that traditionalists are just as adept as the so-called liberals at picking and choosing which bits of Church teaching are to their taste. Maybe being a cafeteria Catholic is just a state of being.

The present not-so-loyal opposition argues that "error has no rights," which masks an inclination to a creeping infallibility that forecloses debate on issues about which there is legitimate disagreement. This has serious pastoral fallout at the grassroots. Indeed, one gets the sense that the ecclesial house of cards of these dissenters is very shaky—give any ground on anything and the entire structure will come tumbling down.

The bottom line for Christians is that every person has rights, even those who hold what we might believe is an erroneous position: the right to dignity; to respect; to charity; and to being listened to and interpreted with generosity. If we fail to honor these rights, the evil one is certainly not far away.

Sadly, for Christians, as for those of other faiths and even those with no faith in God, I fear that our way of proceeding is often to close down discussion and debate. We seem unable to have respectful disagreements with each other. Saints Peter and Paul managed it, and so should we.

The days of seeing Catholics as needing to be protected from "confusion" are over. We are intelligent enough to be able to sort the wheat from the chaff every day in other spheres of our lives. It's not by accident that the oldest Christian rule of discernment is the *sensus fidei.* It is time to trust it again.

The issue of scandal is real. But it is not theologians searching honestly for complex answers to real life issues in the light of the best studies in Scripture, theology, psychology, science, and Catholic experience that is the scandal. Scandal is alive and well in the Church whenever we fail to practice what Jesus preached about: sacrificially loving all our brothers and sisters; when we fail to live simply and humbly, or to act justly, or put "the little ones" first.

Scandal

When Jesus spoke of "scandal" he used the word *skandalon*, meaning a stumbling block placed in the way of the blind.

What the Church might need now more than ever is the eyes to see afresh the complex world to which Christ has sent us, rather than the simpler one in which we would prefer to evangelize. Perhaps this a time to stop confusing unity with uniformity, to be loyal to Christ's law of love, and to confront the real scandals that have seen our moral credibility and our relevance seriously questioned.

31

RITUAL MATTERS

Civic rituals have been gaining momentum since the Enlightenment. The godfather of sociology, Emile Durkheim, was a pioneer in demonstrating that all societies needed shared rituals to affirm their common identity.

For millennia, religious collectives provided these rituals, but since the eighteenth century, nation states have had to provide secular events separated from explicit references to religious myths, doctrines, and liturgy to affirm a national and international collectivity.

Some of these civic rituals may have religious foundations but have taken on a life of their own with little or no connection to the original event, such as Christmas and Thanksgiving in North America.

Even when theists point out that the atheistic regimes of the Soviet Union, communist China, Nazism, and Pol Pot accounted for 1.2 billion deaths in the twentieth century, atheist scholars like Sam Harris unconvincingly argued that the problem with these deadly systems was that they were too religious in ritual, dogma, and personality cult.

Regardless of their origins—from family naming ceremonies, baptisms, weddings, and funerals to World Youth Day, the Olympics, and the Paralympics—ritual matters.

In trying to describe the importance of these rituals, some cultural theorists use the term *event drama*—the theory that with the decrease of daily, weekly, or regular religious rituals in secular societies, these events, even if they have some religious element to them, have taken on an even greater personal and social importance.

The extraordinary amount of money now generally spent on everything to do with the Olympics and the Paralympics is increasingly hard to justify for the celebration of sport and the national feel-good factor. The same can be said for many weddings in developed countries, where I know families who mortgage their houses to host the event.

It would be helpful to see a transparent study on how much World Youth Day has cost the host diocese. While it has had a clear and manifestly good impact on the personal lives and faith of some young adults, sadly I know a much greater number for whom it was a great show that seems to have had little discernible immediate impact on the practice of their faith, their social outreach, or personal spirituality. In this sense, World Youth Day seems to have become an expensive Catholic "event drama."

PART FOUR

FAITH

THE FEAST

A creative way of celebrating the Feast of the Most Holy Body and Blood of the Lord might be to watch *Babette's Feast*. This 1986 film is one of the finest contemporary parables about the Eucharist that I know. While it can be equally read as a homage to an artist, the sacramental reading is fascinating.

Based on Karen Blixen's (writing as Isak Dinesen) novel of the same name, Babette, a French Catholic, is a Parisian chef who gets caught up in the riots in the French capital in 1871. Her husband and son are killed in the fighting. Babette is assisted to escape to Norway (Denmark in the film), where members of a strict Protestant sect take her into their remote village. The founder of the community has died, but his two daughters engage Babette as their cook. The mysterious woman assumes the nature of a servant. They have no idea who she is or what has bought her to their home. Having been in the village for fourteen years, Babette wins ten thousand francs in the lottery and asks the sisters to let her provide a feast in honor of what would have been their father and the pastor's hundredth birthday. She spends all her winnings on buying food and wine so that she can provide a banquet for the community who saved her life.

On the night of the meal, the members of the starkly Protestant community are anxious about the food and wine they will be served. They have never had such rich fare before and have never tasted alcohol. They decide to eat the feast that Babette has prepared but to draw no attention to it, offering up their meal as reparation for sin. Also present at the feast is a local man who is now a general in the army. While he can't understand how the villagers can ignore the beauty of the meal, he notes that the only time he has had such fare was at the Café Anglais from the hands of Paris's most celebrated chef, a woman. Babette remains unseen throughout the dinner, but despite their resistance, her meal has a dramatic effect on the diners.

Akin to the secrecy of Jesus's identity in Mark's Gospel, Babette's full story is only gradually revealed, and even then, it is not fully disclosed. Like Mary and Martha of Bethany, the sisters welcome their guest in her need and out of their Christian devotion. Laboring away in hiddenness, Babette comes into her own through powers beyond the world of the village: the lottery. Then, she can plan and execute the anniversary meal, the one she longed to share. She pours all she has into the meal. This last point is worth amplifying. The sisters who've come to rely on her expect that, with her newfound fortune, Babette will abandon them. Having become poor, however, she remains faithful to them until the end. Babette may not give her physical life for her people but dies to her old life and is reborn as a slave.

The Feast

The feast is one of the great metaphors Jesus used to describe his kingdom, where the best of everything is provided for the rich and poor alike. But it is the effect of this meal that most reveals its nature. There are twelve diners around the table and most of them do not understand the significance of the meal. Only one diner, the general—possibly a priest for the unseen host—can interpret the signs and fully appreciate the fare placed before them. At this meal, the truth is told, forgiveness is granted, and a more unified community emerges.

Channeling Babette, one of my professors of liturgy once told our class, "If you can't, or don't know how to host a dinner party, you have no right to preside at the Eucharist." Though the analogy can be taken too far, he was making the point that, in Christ's name, the presider should prepare the space, attend to all the details in advance, create a hospitable environment, welcome the assembly, enable them to hear the story and share their own, create a community from the congregating individuals, and send them out fed, refreshed, and encouraged.

Whether we interpret Babette as an artist or a Christ figure, this film narrates how a meal can sometimes transform our lives. Christians hold that the eucharistic meal, from which we celebrate the Feast of Corpus Christi, both changes lives here and now, and prefigures the eternal banquet to come. That is why "it's the Mass that matters"—then, now, and for eternity to come.

33

AN ANNIVERSARY

Recently, I celebrated the thirtieth anniversary of my priestly ordination. This moment gives cause for sober reflection on what has happened in the intervening years, gratitude for the many blessings, and resolve about what is still to come.

When I was ordained, Elizabeth II had been queen of Australia for forty-one years and Paul Keating was her prime minister. Bill Clinton was the president of the United States and John Major was the prime minister of the United Kingdom. The Bosnian War was raging. That year, Nelson Mandela and F. W. de Klerk won the Nobel Peace Prize; the Maastricht Treaty formally established the European Union; and Yitzhak Rabin and Yasser Arafat signed a peace agreement on the White House lawn.

Furthermore, the IRA exploded a huge bomb in the heart of the City of London and Islamist fundamentalists attacked the World Trade Center. Two Los Angeles Police Department officers were convicted of violently beating Rodney King. The World Health Organization (WHO) estimated that fourteen million people were living with the

AIDS virus, and a human embryo was cloned for the first time in the United States.

Ben Johnson was banned from athletics for life for doping. *Schindler's List* was the biggest film in the world, and Whitney Houston was belting out "I Will Always Love You." And probably most importantly, the World Wide Web was launched for free from CERN in Switzerland.

After fifteen years in office, Pope John Paul II was in his prime, traversing the globe as the universal pastor. He issued what would become his last encyclical, *Veritatis Splendor*, on the Church's moral teaching. He formally apologized for the Church's role in the African slave trade and would soon publish *Ordinatio Sacredolatis*, restating that the priesthood is for men alone and that no more discussion on the matter would be permitted. In 1994, he would be *Time* magazine's "Man of the Year."

Most telling of all for the Church, in the early 1990s, clerical sexual abuse was starting to be investigated and reported, though most people within the Church thought that these were one-off instances of criminal behavior from aberrant men, not the first signs of the systematic and criminal dysfunction we later saw uncovered.

The idea of a jubilee as we celebrate it today comes from the Old Testament. The root of the word is from the Hebrew word *yobhel*, which refers to the ram's horn that sounded all over Israel to usher in the Jubilee Year. In biblical times, most people were dead by the age of fifty, so a Jubilee Year was a once in a lifetime event often marked by three major events: slaves were set free; the fields were allowed to go fallow for a year; and debts were forgiven.

Through the crucible of the last few years, I think the voice of the faithful is being set free in a way we have never witnessed. On so many levels, those people who have remained with us are, like Howard Beale in the film *Network*, "as mad as hell and are not going to take this anymore!" I think the best clerics have been set free, too, from a misplaced loyalty to the institution over truth, transparency, justice, and love.

The outcome of the fields being left fallow was that the regenerated soil brought forth an even greater harvest. Pope Francis has placed the care of creation at the center of his papacy, as the great right-to-life issue of our time, but even more, he has challenged us to live the gospel with joy, even in the hard times, so that we will continue to sustain and nurture each other.

And then to the forgiveness of debts. Rather than seeing ourselves as the dispensers of mercy, the Church has been humbled by God to recognize that we need to make many more apologies and many more sincere amendments to our lives before we can begin to regain our moral credibility. There is no resurrection without the cross!

Even over these past twenty-five conflicted years, I can honestly say that I have loved being a priest. Not that every day has been delirious. There have been moments when I have seriously thought about leaving. Even though we know the great good the Church does every single day around the world, like many of you, I have been, at various times, ashamed, angry, grief-filled, and alienated.

But whenever I conducted a baptism, presided at the Eucharist, celebrated Christ's mercy, witnessed a marriage, anointed the sick, buried the dead, received someone into the Church, or preached, taught, or wrote about the faith, I knew I was in the right place, doing the right thing. It is a profound privilege for which I am immensely grateful.

And I am excited about what the next twenty-five years of ministry will be like for all of us. Let's decide to be more faithful, more hopeful, and more loving. A jubilee prayer: for all that has been, thank you; and for all that is to come, O God....Yes. Amen.

34

SAINTS PETER
AND PAUL

Priests are often ordained on or around June 29, because it is the Feast Day of Saints Peter and Paul. It is incredible to think that two of the most important saints in the Christian calendar share a feast day. We could easily have doubled our money by having a separate day for each of them. Traditionally, we say that Peter and Paul symbolize two facets of Christianity: mission and maintenance. Paul is the great missionary and Peter the great leader who held the earliest disciples together. The only problem with this evenly balanced paradigm is that it overlooks the fact that Peter was also a great missionary, and Paul was also a master maintainer.

Though both were crucial to the early Christian community's survival and expansion, it's their worst moments that may have the most to teach us. Peter's infamous denial gives comfort to any of us who ever in a moment of weakness chose self-preservation over being faithful. This uneducated, brash, and impulsive man was, in the end, to give the greatest witness to faith in Christ, but it came through the tears of having betrayed—not once but three times—the one who had loved him and who had called him his "rock."

And even after having been forgiven and having assumed the leadership of the nascent Church, Peter still does not seem to get who Christ's kingdom is for—everyone. When it came to preaching the gospel to the Gentiles and to adapting the demands of the Jewish law regarding new Christians, Peter was slow to the party. But he was humble enough to admit that he was wrong. In the end, he got with the program; he ended up dying for it.

Paul is an even more complex character. I must admit that, in recent years, every time I have heard about religious fanatics doing murderous things in God's name, I think of St. Paul. We have conveniently whitewashed his story. Paul may have been a highly educated lawyer, but he was also a religious fruitcake—a murderous zealot. From Acts 9, Philippians, Galatians, and to a lesser degree, 1 Timothy and 1 Corinthians, we know that this self-confessed "chief among the sinners" went from town to town presiding over the extermination of Christians. No wonder the earliest disciples were wary of him and of his dramatic conversion from being an extreme Jewish nationalist to the greatest of Christian missionaries.

In both Peter and Paul, but in different and equally rewarding ways, we can celebrate the truth of that old dictum: "It doesn't matter how you start, but how you finish." Rather than sanitize their stories of failure and brutality, I find comfort in their warts-and-all histories that eventually end in giving glory to him whose power working in them could do infinitely more than they could ever ask or imagine. It also puts paid to the idea that the Church has ever been a community of the pure of heart. Peter and Paul were loved sinners whose conversions to Christ were hard won and took time. Just like us.

Maybe it is Peter and Paul's most celebrated clash that remains the most instructive for us. As important as other councils have been in the life of the Church, the Council of Jerusalem was arguably the most important the Church has ever had. At issue was whether Gentiles had to become Jews before converting to Christianity—in particular, whether men who wanted to become Christians first had to be circumcised—and whether Gentiles had to observe the law of Moses after their conversion. The decisions the Council made would be decisive for the mission of the early Church.

Peter and Paul disagreed. And they did not pull any punches. But they seemed to have been able to do what many in the Church today can't do—to disagree *respectfully*. Ideology is the enemy of true discernment. It predestines the outcome to every conversation, cuts across a spirit of curiosity and humility toward new opportunities and leaves no room for the Holy Spirit to prompt and move us to new responses to new contexts and issues. Peter and Paul's fundamental change of heart may not have been to a greater commitment to Christ, but to becoming adaptable and able to compromise on things that were not essential to salvation.

So, there is great wisdom in having ordinations to the priesthood around the joint feast day of these unlikely Christian heroes. After confronting their hearts of darkness, overcoming their fears, staring down the instinct for self-preservation, and then experiencing the freedom of Christ, and receiving the community's forgiveness,

Peter and Paul became role models of humility, flexibility, and trust in the Lord. They knew they did not have all the answers, but along with the whole community, they became seekers of where the Spirit was leading.

We have never needed their witness more than now.

35

CHRIST THE KING

Recently, I saw the digitally reworked film of the late Queen Elizabeth II's coronation. This was British ritual at its most brilliant. The sense of flow, dignity, and beauty was overwhelming. I was struck by how this rite mirrored the ordination of a bishop. It has a call, oaths, the reception of the Scriptures, the Liturgy of the Word, recitation of the Creed, an anointing, the presentation of the symbols of office leading up to the crowning, the acclamation by the people, an enthroning, the homage of the subjects, holy communion, the *Te Deum*, and finally, the recessional. It was made explicitly clear that Christ was anointing Elizabeth Alexandra Mary "to govern the Peoples of the United Kingdom of Great Britain and Northern Ireland, Canada, Australia, New Zealand, the Union of South Africa, Pakistan, and Ceylon, and of your Possessions and the other Territories."

The camera then panned around Westminster Abbey—dukes and duchesses, earls and countesses, anyone who is anyone was there. As I watched, however, I became increasingly uncomfortable. While everything was said to be done in Christ's name, I could only think that Christ would prefer to be anywhere but here. For millennia, in ceremonies like this all around the world, Christ's kingship is often called upon to confirm that God approves of not only this particular monarch or that particular president, but also of the entire social, economic, and religious hierarchy that seems to go with the institution of the state.

Following on from Jesus saying he was a king, "but not of this world," Christians celebrated his reign as that of the Messiah, or the Christ, literally, "the anointed one," the Redeemer King, who would defend the rights of the poor and establish an everlasting reign of justice and peace. The notion of Jesus as an earthly king and an anointer of earthly kingdoms came with the conversion of Emperor Constantine in 313. Bishops started to wear the magenta robes of the senators, churches took on the shape of Roman basilicas, while the government of the Church came to mirror that of the empire. The Christian liturgy imported all sorts of practices popular in the Roman temples and in civic rituals. Within a century, Christian art began to depict Jesus dressed in royal robes, with a crown, a scepter, and an orb. Mary is often presented in similar dress and begins to be called the Queen of Heaven; by the high medieval period, she is often cloaked in blue, the prerogative of kings at the time.

We cannot change history, but we do not have to be trapped by it either. In the very Scriptures given into our monarch's hands, we discover Christ our King is not found among earthly wealth and splendor, but in desperate poverty, in homelessness, in seeking out and saving the lost, in getting down and getting dirty in the service of those who live on the margins of society. I am not convinced such groups would be welcome or at home in the lavish coronation ceremonies conducted in Christ the King's name in the Westminster Abbeys of our world.

If we take Christ's kingship seriously, we cannot delude ourselves into understanding it in terms of worldly status. Jesus said that "whoever wants to be first must be last of all and servant of all" (see Mark 9:35). I admire the lifetime of privileged service that Queen Elizabeth rendered during her reign and her obvious and sincere Christian faith, but Christ does not anoint any social or ecclesiastical system of privilege and wealth that is extravagant or disordered in its social relationships.

The most moving moment when Jesus speaks of his kingship is from the cross, when the good thief simply asks, "Jesus, remember me" (see Luke 23:33–43). Jesus replies that being remembered by God *is* paradise. The power of Christ the King is seen in his memory, in holding every person in this world close, in calling each one of us by name and challenging us to live lives of sacrificial love. It is seen where simplicity is valued, and where there is a right relationship with the earth. It is seen where the poor are recognized as special points of God's revelation to the world.

The test of those who live out the reign of Christ is not whether we are monied or titled, whether we are successful, or have made it as an entry in *Who's Who*. Christ our King calls us to follow him in remembering all people, regardless of who they are, and being prepared to pay the price in fighting for the dignity of each person. And what's our reward for bringing Christ's reign to bear in our world? That Christ will remember us when we come into his kingdom.

36

SALVE REGINA

On August 15, 1975, the entire parish council of a village a few hours' travel from Santiago, the capital of Chile, was arrested by the military police. For months, the other villagers tried to find out where the men had gone and why. Abduction, torture, and illegal imprisonment were daily realities under the regime of General Augusto Pinochet.

Word finally arrived in November that the corpses of each of the councilors could be found in Santiago's morgue. My friend, Catherine, a religious sister, was working in the parish. She drove the mothers of the eight men to the morgue. Catherine later wrote to me:

> You could not imagine what we found in the morgue. There were over a hundred corpses piled high on each other, and each mother had to roll someone else's son over to find her own. And as the mothers searched, they began to weep loudly, realizing how evil we can be

toward one another. As they wept, they prayed the rosary. As one mother, and then another, found her son, they called out more desperately, "Holy Mary, Mother of God. Pray for us sinners now, and at the hour of our death."

Catherine's letter continued:

For years, I rejected devotion to Mary because I felt oppressed by the way generations of men in the Church presented her—blue veils, white skin, always smiling, a perpetual virgin and yet also a mother, an ideal I could never achieve, but one to which I was told I should aspire. In the experience of the village mothers, however, the distortions of who Mary was for a poor and suffering world faded away. Far from feeling distant from their devotion, I found myself praying with them, knowing that Mary was with us in our shock, anger, and grief.

Catherine then went on to describe their journey home:

It was harrowing. My pickup truck could not take all the mothers and their sons in the back, so I had one of them in the front with me, cradling her son in her arms all the way back to our village. I asked on the long trip home about their prayer to Mary. She said, "We can only pray with Mary at times like this because she knows what it's like to bring a child into the world and claim his dead body in her arms."

In 1989, Catherine died of hepatitis. Her family had been trying to get her to come back to Australia for months, but after twenty-five years that village in Chile had become home. Soon after, the family received a letter from the mothers in the village. When it was translated into English it read,

> We want you to know that we were with Sister Catherine when she died. We would never have let her die alone for she was one of our children, too. We often prayed the rosary with her in recent weeks. She seemed to like that, thumbing the beads she used ever since she brought us back with our boys. We have buried her next to our sons and put on her tombstone the line she asked us to inscribe: "Mary, my friend, my companion and mother of the poor, pray for me."

In 2001, I attended a conference in Chile. On our only day off, I caught a bus into the mountain range behind Santiago. Nearly three hours later, I alighted in the village in the noonday sun. Six surviving mothers greeted me like a long-lost son and took me to Catherine's grave, which was immediately adjacent to those of their sons. We stood. We wept. We embraced. One of them asked me to pray. I don't speak Spanish, and they spoke little English. Then I began singing that ancient Latin love song in honor of Our Lady: *Salve Regina*. And as soon as I started, they all joined in. Something was reborn in me that day and it has flourished ever since.

Now is not the time for us to throw out devotion to Mary, but to reclaim a relationship with her under

FAITH

whatever title works best: *mother, first among the saints, prophet, friend, companion in faith.* If we are in touch with the fact that we are poor in spirit, we know she meets us there and always journeys with us to her Son: now, and at the hour of our death.

37

BE THE MIRACLE

Almost every time there is a beatification or a canonization, the requirement for a physical miracle comes under scrutiny. It happened with St. Mary Mackillop, St. John Henry Newman, and more recently with St. John Paul II. There are those who argue that the demand for a physical healing is too narrow. In Dublin, the intercession of the saintly Matt Talbot may not have produced too many cures from cancer, but there are hundreds of people who attest that through his intercession their loved ones have come to sobriety and remained so. Anyone who has lived with a chronic alcoholic can appreciate the miracle of this transformation. Conversely, there are others who hold that, if God is going to perform miracles through the intercession of prospective saints, we do not just need a cure here and there for a blessed few, we need many more miracles for everyone.

Miracles raise issues regarding the degree to which God intervenes in our lives and acts in a way that appears inconsistent with the laws of nature that, under God's care, have been set in place. They also challenge our concept of prayer, especially the efficacy of petitionary prayer, both here on earth and in heaven.

This interest is not a fascinating abstraction for me. It is personal. As a result of a car accident many years ago, my sister was left a quadriplegic. I prayed, fasted, begged, and wept for a miracle for her. None came.

That miracles occur seem to me to be beyond dispute, especially in the realm of physical, emotional, or spiritual healing. In classic Christian dogma, the believer is required to affirm that miracles happen and that the author of the miracle is God. I can do both easily. I do not, however, believe that they come from without. I believe God works miracles from within. I have no concept of God "zapping" people with miraculous power. Such an idea can reduce God to a magician, gaining the admiration of the spellbound audience who long to see his next amazing trick. One of the many problems with this model is that the most deserving people I know, like my sister, never seem to be called up on celestial stage. I also reject this "magic model" because I cannot find it in the actions of Jesus. "Sign faith" in John's Gospel was considered the weakest faith of all. Furthermore, if miracles were simply a question of God's power, then why could Jesus not perform miracles always and everywhere? The writers of the Gospels often put it down to a "lack of faith," which already allows for other preconditions for a miracle to occur.

Contemporary neuroscience is beginning to understand the general properties of the brain and its potential to heal. Miracles occur when some of these healing assets are released by the brain into the body. For some, the reception of the anointing of the sick and the laying on of hands unlocks these properties. For others, it may be a pilgrimage to a holy place, personal or intercessory prayer, or a devotion to a saint. For other more secular people I know who have experienced a miracle, it was a complete change in lifestyle, diet, and the practice of meditation.

This goes some way toward explaining why Jesus could perform some miracles and not others and why, at Bethsaida, Jesus had to have a second go at healing the man born blind. Even an encounter with Jesus or a single touch was not enough for some people, while for others their master's or friend's desires to see them well was enough to affect the change. Given that Christians readily concede that the evolution of the human brain is among God's greatest handiwork, then God is, in every sense, the author of the miraculous.

It is just a question of where God's grace resides. It is not just from without. Brian Doyle, in his chapter "Grace Notes" in *Leaping: Revelations and Epiphanies*, captures the same sense: "We think of grace arriving like an ambulance, a just-in-time delivery, an invisible divine cavalry cresting a hill of troubles, a bolt of jazz from the glittering horn of the creator, but maybe it lives in us and is activated by illness of the spirit. Maybe we're loaded with grace. Maybe we're stuffed with the stuff."

So, what of the efficacy of prayer? We believe that our prayer follows the categories of the Psalms: lamenting our situation, that is to cry out in anguish; giving thanks and praise; affirming our trust and faith; singing of our salvation; simply waiting upon the presence of God; and petitioning God. I think the most common form of address from humanity to God is the last one, asking for something to happen to someone somewhere.

Problems only arise when our prayers are not answered. Then, it can be said that we were asking for the wrong thing, that God said no, or answered the real need that we may not have known was more important. It can also be said that we did not do enough prayer or the right type of prayer in the right way. We can think that if we had fasted more or undertaken more penance, God would have come down on my side. This model can easily reduce the God and Father of Jesus Christ to Zeus.

Zeus was not an easy god with whom to get along. One of the lessons other gods and mortals learned quickly was that, if you wanted your petitions granted, you had to stay on Zeus's good side. As with all the Greek gods, sacrifice and prayer were the usual offerings. The hierarchy of sacrifices and the length of prayers seem to have been in relation to how much a petitioner wanted Zeus to listen to the plea, change his mind, or be kind to him or her.

But the God and Father of Jesus Christ is not Zeus. Our prayer is not about asking or telling God what to do and to get him to change his mind. The traditional Christian doctrine of immutability holds that God, in his essence, is unchanging. This was a defining break with Greek and Roman theology, and a development from the God in some parts of the Old Testament. God's unchanging nature is essential for the sake of our relationship with him and our sanity. This affects our prayer. I believe that all the sacrifices and prayers in the world cannot change God because that is the way God wants it. The Apostle James writes, "Every generous act of giving, with every perfect gift, is from above, coming down from the Father of lights, with whom there is no variation or shadow due to change" (Jas 1:17).

So, what does our petitionary prayer do? Why bother praying to a God who does not change? When we pray, we are asking our holy, loving, and unchanging God to change us, and thereby change the world. Our fasts, penances, sacrifices, and prayers can help change us, to be more open and receptive to God's love and life, which is constantly available.

I have no problem believing that our companions in heaven, the saints, continue to pray that we might allow God to change us so that, in the power of God's grace, we can change the world. Sometimes when this happens the result is miraculous.

The writers of the film *Bruce Almighty* were inspired when they placed these words on the lips of God:

> Parting your soup is not a miracle, Bruce, it's a magic trick. A single mom who's working two jobs, and still finds time to take her son to soccer practice, that's a miracle. A teenager who says no to drugs and yes to an education, that's a miracle. People want me to do every-thing for them. What they don't realize is they have the power. You want to see a miracle, son? Be the miracle.

38

THE SACRED HEART

Because the people of the ancient world could feel their hearts beat, and see it move, and they knew that when it stopped people died, they believed that the heart rather than the brain controlled the body. Understandably, in this prescientific world, the heart was given mystical properties.

Even today we still talk about people who have "big, good, or full hearts," are "warm or broken-hearted," or are "heartless." These metaphorical uses of the word point to a presence or an absence of love. And the best continuing example of this tradition is St. Valentine's Day, from an obscure Roman martyr whose feast day took over a pagan festival of love. It's not by accident that February 14 is covered in hearts.

Every year on June 3, we mark the Solemnity of the Sacred Heart of Jesus. St. Margaret Mary Alacoque is credited with popularizing the Sacred Heart, but the devotion certainly predates her. It's described as early as the eleventh century and recorded in the visions and

writings of many holy men and women, including Ger-
trude, Mechtilde, Frances de Sales, Francis Borgia, and
John Eudes, among others.

Almost always, large-scale public devotions in our
Church rise to counter a theological position. When
St. Margaret Mary had her religious experiences, France
was in the grip of the Jansenist heresy. Among many
other things, Jansenism placed great emphasis on individual responsibility for sin and the difficulty of obtaining
Christ's mercy, whose true humanity was played down.

In this context, Margaret Mary saw that the
wounded, suffering heart of Jesus expresses his love,
intimacy, and forgiveness for us. Part of her revelation
was that the popularizing of this devotion should be
given to the Jesuits, who were also the loudest oppo-
nents of the Jansenists at the time.

The fact that the devotion spread like wildfire in the
latter part of the seventeenth century says something
about how necessary it was for the Church. Ever since,
it has proved incredibly adaptable to the movements of
theology and spirituality that has seen the Church move
away from being driven by fear to being drawn by love.

Devotion to the Sacred Heart of Jesus may have suffered cardiac arrest in recent decades, but only because
Vatican II absorbed the best elements of it: where Jesus's
humanity is celebrated, his suffering and death are seen
as an expression of his love for us, and the Eucharist is
the most intimate of moments where Christ is broken
and poured out in love so that we can reproduce the pat-
tern of his sacrificial love in our own lives.

I must admit that I don't like corporate speak very
much, but the phrase *value-added* is an apt one here. I
am yet to be convinced that the devotion to Divine Mercy

adds any value to the already venerable devotion to the Sacred Heart.

Maybe it's because I am a Jesuit; maybe it's because as much as I dislike some former representations of the Sacred Heart, the ever-multiplying Divine Mercy painting does little to inspire me theologically or artistically. And while I know some people who find comfort in this recent devotion, I have mixed feelings about it taking over the Second Sunday of Easter and a Divine Mercy novena being recited before it. A solemnity on June 3 is one thing, but a universal takeover of the Church's Easter Triduum and then the most joyous days that follow is quite another.

My major concern is that for those of us who have read St. Faustina's revelations, the theology that emerges there can easily be reduced to a transactional model of grace, where God's forgiveness will not be granted and his anger at our sins will not be wiped away until we do certain actions in the way prescribed.

As it is enshrined and enacted in Divine Mercy, the descriptions of God's forgiveness seem to be at odds with the generous, inclusive, gratuitous, and unmerited theology we are hearing about as we become a more synodal Church.

The devotional life of the Church often reveals as much about us as it does about God. If large-scale public devotions in our Church rise to counter a theological position, then we are witnessing a quiet battle right now: from being drawn by love to again being driven by fear.

I hold firm to the contemporary image and theology of the Sacred Heart that enshrines an ancient metaphor to remind us of a God who jealously regards us as his own, is incomprehensibly loving and compassionate, and calls us to be likewise to everyone we meet.

39

MARY MAGDALENE

Mary Magdalene should sue the Church for defamation. Whatever of her being the apostle to the apostles on Easter Day, since Tertullian in the third century, her name has been synonymous with being a woman in prostitution. She is not the other women in the Gospels who "have a bad reputation in the town," or "weep at Jesus's feet and wipe their tears away with their hair," or are caught in the "very act of adultery," or pour oil over Jesus's head.

The first we hear of Mary Magdalene is that she has seven demons cast out of her by Jesus. We're not told what these demons are, but given what people wrongly thought at the time, they could have been a tummy complaint, acne, or a twitch. There is no suggestion they were sexual demons.

The stage performance *Jesus Christ Superstar* didn't do Mary's saucy notoriety any favors by giving her the song of the show: "I Don't Know How to Love Him."

FAITH

Curiously some brides want this song sung at their weddings, to which I reply, "If you don't, you shouldn't be here." And think of the rest of the song's chorus: "And I've had so many men before, in very many ways...he's just one more."

I don't think that's what we want to say at a Nuptial Mass!

The most important thing we know about Mary Magdalene is that, in three of the four Gospels, she is the first to experience the risen Christ and is the first Christian missionary, the apostle to the apostles.

Two details in John's account are especially poignant. We are told that Mary encountered the risen Christ while weeping outside Jesus's tomb. She felt a double loss on that first Easter Sunday. Not only was she grieving for the loss of the one whom she had seen tortured to death, but she also wept for what she thought was the ultimate insult inflicted on him—the desecration of his grave and the stealing of his corpse.

Mary Magdalene is the patron saint of all who have ever stood at tombs and wept. Furthermore, she shows us that, amid any grief, Christ comes to us and calls by name. Because of Mary's tears and even more because of her evangelization, we believe that there is not a human being who is not known to God by name. Jesus tells Mary that his God and Father is now her God and Father. God makes no distinction between anyone; we are all called by name to share in his life according to the grace which enables us to do so. God not only knows our name; he knows our heart, our history, and our selves.

In the Easter accounts Mary Magdalene is the first "witness" to the resurrection. For us, the word *witness* usually means that we attest to the truth of events from personal experience and knowledge. The power of personal witness can hardly be exaggerated.

The same is true of Christian faith today. It might be attractive to believe in Jesus Christ as Savior of the world as a good idea or as an engaging concept. But the best witnesses have firsthand access to the truth. They don't believe in the idea of the resurrection but have had a personal encounter with the risen Christ themselves and are bold enough to proclaim and live it.

This may be why in the early Church the word for witness and the word for martyr were one and the same. Anyone who was brave enough to witness publicly to the resurrection at that time potentially ended up giving his or her life for it. This a compelling argument for the reality of the resurrection.

Within a generation after Jesus's death, people all over the Mediterranean world, most of whom had never seen Jesus, reported that they too had encountered the presence of the risen Christ—that Jesus of Nazareth was not dead but alive to them, too, and these same people not only believed in the resurrection, but they were also prepared to put their lives on the line for the person they had encountered.

Nothing has changed. At Easter, we are called to be witnesses to Jesus, raised from the dead, and alive to us here and now. This is no head trip, for in our own way we are meant to put our bodies on the line for it.

Like Mary Magdalene, in our witness to Christ, we will have to pay a price for how we live and whom we challenge.

40

A PILGRIMAGE OF FAITH

The season of Lent is often described as a "pilgrimage of faith." Pilgrimages have always been alluring for Christian believers. My most stark experience of being sent out as a pilgrim did not happen very far from home. When I was in the Jesuit novitiate in the mid-1980s, the second-year novices were dropped 125 miles (200 kilometers) walk from our first house in Australia at Sevenhill, in the Clare Valley north of Adelaide, South Australia. The Austrian Jesuits founded it in 1850. It is, to this day, a parish, retreat house, and, thank God, it's a very fine winery!

We were given enough money for one emergency phone call and a letter from the novice master for the police explaining who we were and what we were doing. We were, officially, vagrants. With a backpack and a sleeping bag, we had to walk the entire way, begging each day for our food and accommodation. In the pursuit of board and lodging we could not tell anyone who we were nor what we were doing. We could not trade off being a Jesuit. The novice master told us that if we were invited into someone's home, then after we had established the extent of their hospitality, we could tell them who we were so that they would not be frightened that they have welcomed Jack the Ripper to stay the night. If the homeowner, however, offered the garage and a sandwich and then found out that we were Jesuits and then wanted to offer the guest suite and a meal at the dining room table, we were told that an upgrade from economy to first class was not allowed!

Those ten days were the only time in my life I've known hunger. During winter, would you let me into your house, let me sleep in your garage, or give me some food? I stayed in hostels for homeless men run by the St. Vincent de Paul Society, broke into broken-down schoolhouses, camped out at bandstands, and slept out under the stars.

On the sixth day, I arrived in the teeming rain in a small country town at 7:00 p.m. I was soaked to the skin. I was drawn by the bright fluorescent cross that hung over what I was soon to discover was the Catholic Church. There was nothing in the rules to say you could not beg from churches. I walked up to the presbytery steps and introduced myself to the parish priest. After giving out my spiel, I asked, "Father, I am wondering if you could get me in touch with the local SVDP?" In his wonderful Irish brogue, he replied, "You're looking at the local Vincent de Paul." So, Father gave me five dollars for dinner and five dollars for breakfast, a towel for a shower, and a bed in the now unused old school room. Because he never let me into the house, I went on my way the next day without telling him who I was and what I was doing.

On the third last day of the pilgrimage, as it is called, I approached the biggest house in the small town of Riverton. There I met Mrs. Mary Byrne, who proceeded to grill me about where I had come from, why I was in such need, and where I was going. I never told a lie, but I was Jesuitical with the truth. After the interrogation, she declared, "I think I can trust ya," and ushered me into her home. She told me that I could stay in the guest room, have dinner that night and breakfast in the morning, and then be on my way. I then told Mary who I was and what I was doing. To which she said, "Get outta here!" and for a moment I thought she literally meant I had to get out of there. But Mary quickly went on, "The Jesuits look after the church here from Sevenhill." And then she changed, "You haven't been sent out as a spy, have you?"

"No," I said, "Why would you think I've been sent out as spy?"

"Well, you Jesuits are always going on caring for the poor and a faith that does justice in the world, and I thought you lot may have been sent out to spy on us to test whether we have been listening to all those social justice sermons all these years." I assured her I hadn't.

I had a great night with all Mary's family, and the next day I was on my way. When I got to the next small hamlet of Watervale in the late Sunday afternoon, I discovered that everyone was watching or playing the local football competition. The only person I could see was on the rise of the hill on the edge of town where a woman was weeding her front garden beds. I walked up the hill and through her gate and gave out my spiel: "Hello, I'm

Richard Leonard and I am on my way to Clare to get some work at one of the wineries to get my passage back to Sydney. I have nowhere to stay and nothing to eat, and I'm wondering if you can help me with either or both?"

At the end of my speech, the woman looked up from her garden and said, "Are you the Jesuit who stayed with Mary Byrne last night? Her daughter is engaged to my son, and I play the organ at Sevenhill Church." And that night the Byrne family came down and joined me and the Briskys for another wonderful dinner in the Riesling Valley of Australia. Being on pilgrimage was looking good.

When I got to Sevenhill, I wrote back to that generous pastor telling him that, although he did not know it, he had been kind to a Jesuit novice. A short while later a note arrived from the good pastor that read, "The Jesuits taught me at school in Ireland. I hated every single minute of it. If I'd known who you were and what you were up to, I would have kicked your backside and told you to get yourself out of town. Even now, the crafty Jesuits have got one over on me. I knew, however, that there was something a little bit different about you, because, let's face it, you were, without question, the most articulate beggar I've ever met in my life."

On that road to Sevenhill, I learned more about the Lenten journey than at any other time in my life. I discovered that living simply, doing penance and fasting (even if I had no option), being totally dependent on God's goodness through the undeserved kindness of strangers, and being on pilgrimage in the real world helped me feel close to God in a way I had never experienced. I prayed for my daily bread and for somewhere to lay my head, and I was often overwhelmed with gratitude for the smallest kindnesses. While it was a stark context, that pilgrimage showed me that the clutter in my head, heart, and life often gets in the road of me finding God and allowing God to find me.

Even if we do not leave home every year, we do become pilgrims with Christ, and to Christ, every Lent: decluttering as we go through our prayer, penance, fasting, and acts of charity. No matter how soul-sore we may be by journey's end, may this pilgrimage of hope be both life-changing and life-affirming because that's the reward for the pilgrim's progress at Easter.

41

THE FAMILY BURIAL

Among the hardest things a Catholic priest must do is to bury a member of his family. While by law or custom the members of most other professions are discouraged from looking after their own family, a priest is often expected to minister to his. And overall, we want to. Baptisms and weddings are joys. Funerals, though, are tough gigs.

I had to bury my fifty-six-year-old sister, Tracey. I have done many tragic funerals—the deaths of children, the victims of suicide, of car accidents, and murders among them, but Tracey's Requiem Mass was the most demanding of any liturgy at which I have presided. I have acted as the family's priest on other occasions, empathetically pastoral I hope; but now I had to be not just a priest but a grieving brother, personally alive to all the history that had brought us to this day, and alert to all the tensions it held.

Tracey's life and death were more complex than most. After graduating as a nurse in 1981, she immediately left

Australia to work with Mother Teresa in the House of the Dying in Calcutta. All up, she spent three years in India over two stints, and she loved it. On her return home, she ran the health center at Wadeye, a remote aboriginal community in the Northern Territory. *Bush nursing* and *Tracey Leonard* were synonyms.

It was there, aged twenty-eight, on October 23, 1988, while doing a favor for some of her friends, that her car broke down. As it was being towed away, her vehicle rolled off the road and hit a tree. Everyone else got out without a scratch; Tracey was left a quadriplegic. She had been all over the world caring for God's poor; in the twenty-eight years since her tragic accident, Tracey had been the poorest person I know: a kind of poverty that had very little to do with lack of money.

Ten years after the accident, using a voice recognition program, Tracey told the story of her extraordinary experiences in Calcutta and outback Australia. Her book was called *The Full Catastrophe*. Since her death, I have lost count of the number of people who had never met her, but who have told me that they felt they knew her from that book. They found her courage inspiring. I did too.

Whether in or out of a wheelchair, Tracey was passionate about comforting the sick, campaigning for justice—especially for the dignity and rights of indigenous Australians—and defending the innocent. The people who lived out these struggles were her saints—and Tracey was a saint to me.

Saints aren't perfect, but they're transparently good. Tracey was far from perfect, though I have yet to meet anyone who was dealt such a devastatingly cruel hand

and remain as positive, engaged, and encouraging. The evening before she died, after recognizing each of the friends and family who had gathered around her hospital bed, as it seemed her awareness was slipping, she began to call out, "Feed the boat people! Feed the boat people!" While everyone in the room was focused on Tracey's needs, she was focused on those she thought were in greater need still.

In the years after her accident, her death would sometimes be a topic of conversation between us. She gave out lines like "Life has not exactly been all beer and Skittles"; "I don't want to see old bones"; and "You know, Richard, there are worse things than dying." Though she came to some peace and reconciliation with her life, I would not have wanted her to suffer a day longer.

She gave me more than a few instructions for her funeral. Everyone should leave some guidelines as to what they would like. Tracey's went from "Just cremate me quickly like the Hindus do in India" to "I want twenty people in the backyard—and you can say some prayers if you like." Most recently, she pleaded, "I don't care what you do, Richard—just don't go over the top."

I am not sure a Requiem Mass with a bishop and eighteen priests on the altar qualifies as low key, but we did our best to keep it simple. We had the private cremation of her body that she had asked for and the long and wonderful wake that we knew she wanted. These sacred and secular rituals were all deeply consoling.

I lost the plot twice during Mass. The first time was when my brother thanked our almost eighty-four-year-old mother for devotedly caring for our sister over nearly three decades. And I came off the rails again at the very end of my homily. I had decided to adapt the most famous of lines from one of Tracey's favorite saints, Dr. Martin Luther King Jr., and imagined him helping her out of that wheelchair and declaring to the cloud of witnesses, "Free at last! Free at last! Thank God almighty, she's free at last!"

42

WORDS AND WOUNDS

In the Easter season, Thomas makes two notable appearances, one much more significant than the other. The Gospel story about doubting Thomas is one of the most misunderstood episodes in the New Testament.

If you are like me, for years you may have been consoled by Thomas doubting that Jesus had been raised from the dead. We have been told that Thomas doubted Jesus. But if we read the story very carefully, it is not Jesus whom Thomas doubts; it is the disciples. In fact, when Jesus appears to them a week later, Thomas shares in the experience of the risen Lord, and like the others, he immediately confesses Easter faith.

Indeed, Thomas calls Jesus "my lord and my God," which is one the greatest claims made in the Gospels. History has been unfair. He should be confessing Thomas, not doubting Thomas.

There are, however, three elements to this story that should give us great comfort. The first is that Thomas does not doubt Jesus but doubts the early Church, and not just about a minor issue of discipline or procedure. He doubts the central Christian message: that God raised Jesus from the dead. Some of us, too, at various times in our lives, can have doubts about all sorts of aspects of our faith. There are very few believers who get through life without asking some serious questions of God and the Church. These questions are good in themselves and are necessary for a mature, adult faith. What we need to ensure is that we sincerely want to search for answers to these questions. Thomas is the patron saint of all of us who sometimes struggle to believe what everyone else in the Church seems to accept and to have the courage and patience to wait for and seek the answers.

The second consoling fact to this story concerns the earliest Church. Even though they are filled with the presence of the risen Lord, and though Thomas refuses to believe their witness, they remain faithful to him in his doubts. We know this because he is still with them a week later. They didn't expel or excommunicate him from the group; they held on to him in the hope that he would experience the Lord for himself.

Sadly, today, there are some who argue that Catholics who struggle with their faith should "shape up or ship out." While every group has its boundaries, and there are limits from which people can dissent, we could take the earliest Church as our model and stay faithful to our doubters and help them come to see the transforming truth that has changed our lives.

The story of doubting Thomas was written for people like us who do not have access to the historical Jesus. The birth of the Church is an ongoing act of

God's re-creation in every generation. It takes time, and people will be at different stages at different moments.

The third element of the story, even with its mystical details, counters a magical notion of what the resurrection is about. Jesus bears the marks of his torture and death. His glorified body, though radically different, is also in continuity with how the disciples knew and loved him. They can recognize him through his words and his wounds.

The earliest Christian community focused strongly on the wounds of the risen Lord for two reasons: to affirm the fact that Christ, now raised from the dead, was the same person who had lived among them; and to make sense of the physical wounds being inflicted on them for Christ's sake.

Words and wounds still make a claim on us today. We carry within us the death of the Lord. We all have our wounds, and some of the Church's wounds are currently being laid bare very publicly. We also know that, for many of us, it is precisely when we are wounded most deeply by life, that our doubts in the presence of God can be the greatest.

The story of Thomas tells us that Christ can take our fears and doubts and transform them into a powerful Christian witness. Furthermore, the story tells us that where we can only see our woundedness, hopelessness, and death, it is through Easter that faith, hope, and love can have the final word. When we touch our wounds through the wounds of Christ, we may be moved to join in that great Easter cry: "This is the LORD's doing; it is marvelous in our eyes" (Ps 118:23).

43

A "BIRTHING" PARTNER

When I was a seminarian during the long Christmas holidays, I worked in the pastoral care department of a big Catholic public hospital. At a Christmas party, I met the charge nurse of the labor ward. Pleading that, because I was a celibate I would never be at a birth, I inquired if I might be allowed to come and see. The charge nurse thought that would be fine. Six weeks later, I got the call. Apparently, a student priest watching you have a baby is not an easy sell! But Mary was sixteen, had been dumped by her nineteen-year-old boyfriend, and shunned by her family. A kindly seminarian was better than no one at all.

On arrival to the labor ward, I did "ante-natal class 101" in ten minutes: hold Mary's hand; when the midwife tells Mary to "push and keep it coming, keep it coming, keep it coming"—you say it too; don't get in the way; and don't faint!

A "Birthing" Partner

Mary and I met six hours into her labor, which was an unusual circumstance within which to meet your "birthing" partner. She did not have much small talk, maybe because she had no breath. From my vast experience of childbirth, I thought everything was going along swimmingly until the doctor arrived to perform an episiotomy. You don't want to know what that is, and I wish I never did. I swear before God that analgesia would have been invented centuries earlier if men had to go through all of this. We would go on epidurals in the sixth month.

The baby arrived minutes later. Mary wept. She had very good cause to. I wept for no good reason, and the charge nurse wept because I was weeping. There is something so primal and human about the moment of birth that it bonds us to each other. Friendship born in the trenches took on a new meaning for me.

After the tears came the laughter and joy. The reality of Mary's tough situation was happily postponed.

On discharge, Mary asked me to baptize the baby. I couldn't, but I arranged for a priest friend to do it. I am Benjamin Michael's godfather. I have stayed in touch with them for the last thirty years. Mary went on to have three more boys to three different fathers. Tommy, the last dad, is now her devoted husband.

When he was four, I got Benjamin into the local Catholic primary school, where the principal was a Josephite nun, one of St. Mary's MacKillop's sisters. She was formidable but fair. She took an interest in Benjamin and his brothers. Sister only had to go to Mary's home once to demand that the boys get out of bed, were fed, cleaned, dressed, taken to school on time, and later did their homework. It paid off. Sister enrolled all the boys for scholarships to a Christian Brothers High School. On their own merits, each of them won a place. Sister wins a place in heaven. Benjamin is a physiotherapist, Daniel is an accountant, Kai is a social worker, and Noah is a nurse. He has just finished obstetrics. Mary works at the local supermarket. Twenty years ago, I received her and Tommy into the Catholic Church. She now volunteers at the St. Vincent de Paul's local hostel for homeless women. Some of them are sixteen and pregnant.

From a complex conception, a messy birth, a willing midwife, and a vulnerable baby, extraordinary goodness has flowed from one generation to the next. The divine working through human hands at every stage has changed lives. At Christmas, this story comes as no surprise. As noted earlier, in part 2, but worth mentioning again, Rev. John Bell of the Iona Community tells us why:

> Light looked down and saw the darkness.
> "I will go there," said light.
> Peace looked down and saw war.
> "I will go there," said peace.
> Love looked down and saw hatred.
> "I will go there," said love.
>
> So he,
> the Lord of Light,
> the Prince of Peace,
> the King of Love,
> came down and crept in beside us. (Rev. John
>   Bell of the Iona Community, *Cloth for the
>   Cradle*)

44

HER BAGS ARE PACKED

My mother has vascular dementia. Her memory of people and places long past is sharp, but her geriatrician says, "Your mother's brain cannot make new memories." I'd never heard it expressed like that before. It was helpful and freeing. My brother and I had hoped that our mother's final years would be enjoyable and serene. She deserved it. By middle-class standards, Mom has had more than a few heavy crosses to bear. Her own mother died in childbirth when Mom was two years old. She was only married eight years when her thirty-six-year-old husband, my father, had a cerebral berry aneurysm and dropped dead. She was a thirty-two-year-old widow with three children under seven. I was two.

Mom never remarried. "I was a catch, but I had the three of you," she would joke. She never seriously looked for another husband. In 1988, my sister had a catastrophic car accident and became a quadriplegic. Tracey was twenty-eight. Mom was fifty-six. After the best part of a year in the spinal unit, Mom nursed Tracey at home for the next twenty-seven years, rising every night at midnight, 3:00 a.m., and 6:00 a.m. to turn her daughter. Tracey never got a bed sore.

My mother always prayed that Tracey would die first. That prayer was answered quite unexpectedly on March 18, 2017. Mom then prayed that she would die soon afterward: "I've done what I was put on this earth to do. I know you and Peter will be OK and now I'm ready for heaven."

"You're quite confident about where you're going, aren't you?" I'd ask.

"I'd like to see God deny me heaven," was her blunt reply. I would like to see that too.

Mom's prayers to die have not yet been answered, despite my best efforts. On her more lucid days Mom says, "I know I am losing my memory and I'm not enjoying any of this. I hate it. Heaven has to be better than this, so I want you to pray that God will take me tonight." The next day, in an unusual ability to recall a conversation from the day before, Mom says, "Well, your prayers are hopeless, I'm still here."

With gallows humor I reply, "They're going to be answered one day."

Always having the final word, she says, "Well I hope God finds me soon."

Mom's dementia is accelerating dramatically. Because of three falls she had last year, none of which she can remember, she is now in an excellent Catholic aged care facility. Though they look after her beautifully, have Mass and other activities for the residents, after decades of running her home and nursing my sister, Mom is bored to tears.

My mother absconds regularly trying to return to our family home of fifty-three years. We sold it a few months ago. While I admire her spirit to keep trying the great escape, she may have to be transferred into a security ward. Even the idea of that breaks my heart, and, worse still, she cannot process the warnings and the consequences.

The phone is now beyond her. Taking her out for meals is getting harder too. She gets frustrated at not being able to follow the conversation.

Seeing her every day is a blessing, but a mixed one. Some days she's calm with glimpses of her old self back, her quick and sharp wit ready to go. Most days she is confused about where she is, why she's there. The toughest days are when she is resentful and angry at what she perceives we have done to her and demands that we go home—right now. Changing the topic quickly doesn't work.

There is one man at Mom's aged care facility who sits in the common room and calls out loudly all day long, "Help me. Help me." It's a piercing cry. He is the Greek chorus in this human tragedy. No greater number of people have ever lived this long in human history. We are powerless in the face of the ravages of age and as we wait to die.

There is no exclusive patron saint for sufferers of dementia and Alzheimer's. Apparently, they share St. Dymphna, with her primary focus being those who are mentally ill. St. Anthony of Padua is the patron saint of the elderly because he was particularly kind to old people in the thirteenth century. Ironically, he is also the patron saint of finding things.

I think people like my mother, and the growing number of us who will be in this state before we die, need their own patron saint whose only portfolio is to pray with and for them, their families, and the dedicated staff who care for them.

In the meantime, I hope St. Anthony helps God find Mom and take her home because her bags are packed and she's ready to go.

PART FIVE

DISCIPLESHIP

45

THE DISCERNMENT OF SPIRITS

I may be the only Jesuit who will tell you this, but St. Ignatius of Loyola, whose feast day we celebrate on July 31, was an obsessive, compulsive, neurotic nut. That's not fair, of course, because he was also a brilliant, insightful, and deeply holy mystic. However, some of his behavior demonstrates that my comment is neither facetious nor unwarranted.

I want to take you back to 1522, to a cave beside the River Cardoner at Manresa, Spain, where, after dedicating his life to God, Ignatius became a penitent. This was where he had his best and worst days. It was the scene of some very dangerous behavior.

For months, Ignatius whipped himself three times a day, wore an iron girdle, fasted on bread and water for which he begged, slept very little and then on the ground, spent up to seven hours on his knees at prayer, covered his face with dirt, grew his hair and beard rough, and allowed his dirty nails to grow to a grotesque length.

We also know that he suffered from spiritual scruples so badly that he considered committing suicide by throwing himself into the River Cardoner.

Today, we would diagnose Ignatius as being at-risk, a self-harmer, suffering from an acute depressive disorder, and exhibiting suicidal behavior.

Because he had been a soldier, he was used to taking orders from legitimate authorities and following them. When his Dominican confessor saw how Ignatius was mentally and spiritually deteriorating, he ordered him, under holy obedience, to cease all penance immediately and look after himself. He had to obey.

Manresa changed him forever. Not just because he had undergone terrible experiences and lived to tell the tale, but because he reflected carefully on how even good things, like prayer, penance, and fasting, can quickly become instruments of self-destruction. If you or anyone you love has been to a very dark place, here is the saint for you.

In the latter months of his time in that cave, he started writing down his mystical experiences, which became the *Spiritual Exercises*, and he began to formulate his Rules for the Discernment of Spirits. The timeless wisdom in these documents was won in the face of staring down some very destructive demons.

These chapters in St. Ignatius's life give a key to why Ignatian spirituality has been so enduring and adaptable.

Ignatius knew that the spiritual quest starts with our desires—as purified as we must get them. He knew that we often look for all the right things in all the wrong places.

When he emerged from the physical, emotional, and spiritual darkness of that cave, Ignatius knew that the highest goals in life were to follow Christ in being the most loving, hopeful, and faithful person possible.

From hitting rock bottom, he learned that embracing suffering was an inescapable and important moment in coming to grips with our human condition. He also knew that when we try to do this on our own, we can be defeated by isolation and fear. That is why he put such store on the community of faith, in the Church, because he knew that we needed each other and that God was found amid companionship, of being "friends in the Lord."

The combination of systematically reflecting on experience, developing good habits, and being quick to notice and deal with the temptations that lead us astray laid the foundation for Ignatius being "a contemplative in action." His twice daily examen was where he sought to discern the patterns that lead us to God and light, and to keep at bay those patterns that may even look good at first but end up holding nothing but empty promises.

Toward the end of his time at Manresa, again sitting by the river, he had a vision, which he later called his "enlightenment," where he knew he had to go on and out to do great things for God. The River Cardoner went from being his Styx to his Jordan.

Ignatius began his *camino* leaving behind a vain and aimless egotist and finding life, and life abundantly, which involved sixteen years sitting at a desk, founding, and guiding the Jesuits.

DISCIPLESHIP

This extraordinary conversion is enshrined in his Prayer for Generosity, masterfully translated by Daniel Madigan, SJ:

Take hold of me Lord.
Accept this offering of freedom, of memory, of
    mind, of will.
These things I cling to and count as my own.
All are your gifts, Lord, now I am returning
    them.
They are yours. Do as you will.
Give me only your free gift of love.
In this you give all; in this you give all.

46

THE DREAMS OF SAINT JOSEPH

St. Joseph has never had it so good or, at least, he's never had such a friend as in Pope Francis. The pope announced that from December 8, 2020, the Church would celebrate a special Year of St. Joseph. It would honor "the man who goes unnoticed, a daily, discreet and hidden presence, who nonetheless played an incomparable role in the history of salvation." In being tender, open to the demands of faith, obedient, creatively courageous, and humble, St. Joseph is a model for us all, as Pope Francis reminds us.

Devotion to St. Joseph is a comparatively late development in Christian history. We know that, by the ninth century, local churches had commemorations in honor of him as the husband of Mary, but this didn't become a feast day in Western churches until the twelfth century. Only then did devotion to St. Joseph take off. In 1870, Pope Pius XI proclaimed St. Joseph as the Patron of the Universal Church. Almost a century later, Pope

John XXIII added Joseph's name to the first Eucharistic Prayer, and in 2013, Pope Francis extended that directive to Eucharistic Prayers II, III, and IV.

Christian art hasn't been kind to Joseph, usually depicting him as elderly and with the presumption that old men would have no sexual interest in young women. (Those artists need to meet some of the old men I know!) There is nothing in the Gospel texts to indicate that Mary or Joseph were anything other than the marriageable age according to Jewish custom at the time: around thirteen for girls; eighteen for young men.

There are only five episodes involving Joseph in the Gospels: the annunciation; the nativity; the presentation of the child Jesus in the temple; as a refugee to Egypt; and the loss and discovery of the boy Jesus in the temple in Jerusalem. One can see why the early Church may have been slow to make a fuss of him. He is not recorded as ever saying anything in the New Testament—not a word! He should be the patron saint of shy, hardworking, backroom players, who say little but do a lot.

Joseph is a dreamer, that's how God communicates with him. In the Scriptures, his namesake Joseph, the eleventh son of Jacob, is the famous dreamer and interpreter of dreams in the Old Testament. King Nebuchadnezzar, the Prophet Daniel, and King Solomon are just three others whose dreams were to have a dramatic impact on the destiny of Israel. There are plenty of people in the New Testament who also dream dreams and see visions, culminating in the Book of Revelation.

In the Gospels, Joseph has a quartet of dreams: when he is told not to fear taking the pregnant Mary as his wife; when he is warned to flee to Egypt to escape Herod's plan to kill Jesus; when he is given the all-clear to return to Israel; and finally, when he is told not to settle in Judea but to go to Galilee.

Today, we often dismiss belief in dreams as a fad of the new age. This is a mistake. God speaks to us however he needs to. If God has given us an unconscious and subconscious life, of which dreams are a sign, then God has a purpose for this gift, and it can be used for good. Long before Carl Jung, dreams were understood to be a gateway to our inner life and the mystical world, with St. Joseph as their champion. If we refuse to take our dreams seriously, if we decide that God cannot or does not talk to us through our subconscious, then we will never realize their potential.

Even though the flight into Egypt is a theological story, it portrays Joseph's transformation from being a dreamer to being one of history's most famous refugees, fleeing a murderous dictator and saving the Savior of the world.

Just as Matthew draws parallels between the dreams of the Joseph of Genesis with the dreams of Joseph of Galilee, we can also see the parallels in our own lives. Like the Scriptures, dreams need careful interpretation and discernment, but Joseph, the silent partner within the Holy Family, is testament to how a few words and great actions can save ourselves, our family, and even the world.

When Pope Francis announced the Year of St. Joseph, he also gave us a new prayer:

Hail, Guardian of the Redeemer,
Spouse of the Blessed Virgin Mary.
To you God entrusted his only Son;
in you Mary placed her trust;

DISCIPLESHIP

with you Christ became man.
Blessed Joseph, to us too,
show yourself a father
and guide us in the path of life.
Obtain for us grace, mercy, and courage,
and defend us from every evil. Amen.

47

LOVE YOUR NEIGHBOR

Proclaimed in the Letter to the Romans is that whatever other commands there may be, they are "summed up in this word, 'Love your neighbor as yourself'" (Rom 13:9–10).

Some people balk at the words *law* and *love* being used in the same sentence. I understand their hesitation, given that love in its pure sense never comes with conditions attached. It is a gift offered freely. Paul intentionally broke away from thinking of the law of love as obeying a book of rules to seeing it as following Christ who guides all our choices, determinations, decisions, and even sometimes, our duties and responsibilities. It's not a burden but a joyful gift giving. We do not follow laws for their own sake; we follow Jesus Christ.

Sometimes, we hear preachers and teachers say that Judaism, Christianity, and Islam are the "People of the Book." While Judaism does have the Torah, Christians have the Bible, and Islam has the Qur'an, the word

Christians follow is not in a text but in a God who has become flesh and blood. In his autobiographical essay "A Lenten Journey," the Australian Jesuit theologian Daniel Madigan argues that Christians are not people of the Bible, but of God-in-the-flesh: "The divine Word is the energy vibrating within everything that has ever been created (John 1:3). And the language God has chosen in order to speak the Word most fully is the language of our own flesh (John 1:14)—'body language' we might say."[1]

A story highlights Daniel's point. For a couple of years, I was the vocations director for the Australian Jesuits. Early on, I decided that our advertisements needed a makeover, so I asked a friend who owned an advertising agency for some help. Free of charge, he gave me a couple of hours with his creative team, whose job was to brainstorm ideas and create images and words that cut through the crowded marketplace. The group consisted of seven people aged twenty to thirty-five. All arrived late to the session, all wore black, chain-smoked even though there were signs up saying "No Smoking," and generally looked bedraggled. It was 1999. Twenty minutes after the appointed start time, we began, with the leader of the group asking me, "So, Richard, in a sentence or two tell us who the market is and what you're trying to sell."

I was taken aback; this was a new world for me. "Young men between the ages of eighteen to forty who want to give their lives to Christ as a Jesuit in poverty, chastity, and obedience," I replied. After a few moments of stunned silence, the leader dragged heavily on his

---

1. Daniel Madigan, *Christian Lives Given to the Study of Islam* (New York: Fordham University Press, 2012).

cigarette, blew out the smoke and said, "Well, that's the hardest f****** product I've ever had to sell."

We went on to have a very spirited conversation about what the Jesuit life entailed and why someone might choose to live it out today. The group was fascinated and incredulous in equal measure. After two hours, they concluded that what they called my "offering in the marketplace" could not be captured by a pithy slogan or a dramatic visual. We needed an attention-grabbing tagline that would draw those interested to the Australian Jesuits' website, where our vocation could be explored in more depth. And what line did we come up with? *What are you doing on earth for Christ's sake?* The day our new ad campaign was launched, it was all over the national newspapers, and our website crashed.

That night, when I told my Jesuit community about the language the bright young people in the advertising agency had used to describe our vocation, they all roared with laughter. Then, one of the older Jesuits said seriously and truly, "Of course, we aren't *selling* anything. We're offering a way of being in love with Christ, with our sisters and brothers, and with the world."

As the Methodist minister Martyn Atkins once said, "Christians are not meant to be salespeople for the gospel, but we are called to be free samples of it."

Now that's a new take on the law of love. Are we up to being free samples, or loving giveaways, of God's body language?

48

TYRANT OR LOVER

Where the hell was God during the height of the COVID-19 pandemic?

Some Christians have a very limited image of the Holy Trinity: nasty God the Father in heaven; lovely Jesus; and the bird!

While we believe in one God with three personae, they act as one in creating, saving, and inspiring. Furthermore, in John's Gospel, Jesus says that he does nothing on his own (see John 5:30): "the Father and I are one" (John 10:30), and "whoever has seen me has seen the Father" (John 14:9). For a Christian, everything in the Old Testament is interpreted through the definitive revelation of God in Jesus Christ. I know our Jewish sisters and brothers don't like us saying this, but Jesus not only came to fulfill the Old Testament but also to correct it.

This theology matters when we come to plagues and pandemics. For the prescientific peoples of the Bible, everything was given a theological interpretation. If there was a flood, plague, or pestilence, then God was saying something through it. However, in the Gospels, Jesus never sends a plague, a natural disaster, or turns anyone into a pillar of salt, and, for Christians, if Jesus wasn't into murderous retribution, then, if we take him at his repeated word, nor is God. He was the incarnate correction to false interpretations about how God works in the world.

So, even though COVID-19's origins are yet to be finally and scientifically concluded, it has clearly emerged from poor human decisions regarding the created order, not because God has directly sent it upon us.

By contrast, every time there is a local or global catastrophe, there are always those Christian leaders who say that the event has been sent as a punishment by God for various contemporary sins.

This theology reveals a prescientific belief in a tyrannical God, where bad behavior is tolerated up to a point, but then the nonsense is stopped, and a plague is sent to remind us whose boss.

No one loves a tyrant, we survive them as best we can, and in this paradigm, God's love and fidelity seem dependent on what we do, which is a contradiction about the nature of God as revealed in Christ, and in what Paul taught in Romans 8.

God as a tyrant is a fearful, neat solution to the deep pain within our lives: suffering must come from somewhere, and so some argue that it is sent directly by God.

First, there is a huge difference between God permitting evil in our world and God perpetrating such acts upon us. We believe the former tenant, but you would be forgiven for not knowing that we do not hold to the latter one. Because God wanted us to have full freedom, our world had to hold the possibility of choosing evil, non-God, or else we would be marionettes. But this indirect and more general responsibility is a world away from God directly causing suffering and destruction. Just because many people positively grow through the challenges of pain and suffering, it does not mean that God sends these things as a test in the first place. Rather, this growth is a testament to God accompanying us through every moment, inspiring us to be in solidarity with all his children, so that together we make the best decisions in the shadow of death and the valley of tears.

Second, God does not send plagues to teach us things, though we can learn from them, and we are learning much right now about our delicate relationship with the created order and how poor choices in one place can affect all places. We are also learning that the best response in tough times is transparency, good government, honest reporting, collective human ingenuity, responsible citizenship, valuing the common good over individuality, and how extraordinarily resilient some of us are in the face of tragedy.

How can I be so confident that God is not deadly by nature? Because the God revealed in Jesus Christ was not a tyrant but a lover, who was prepared to go to any lengths to save us even though we did not deserve it. Furthermore, John writes that "God is light, in him there is no darkness" (1 John 1:5). If that is true, then plagues cannot be part of God's arsenal of weapons to punish us for our sins in this life.

Spiritual sanity in these difficult days rests in seeing that every moment of every day God does what he did on Good Friday: not allowing evil, death, and destruction to have the last word, but through our humility we see that the power of amazing grace enables us to make the most of even the worst situations, to help each other in every way we can, and to let light and life have the last word. Easter Sunday is God's response to Good Friday: life out of death.

49

LOVE DIVINE

We do not need to go looking for penance. It has visited us with a vengeance: shaming government reports and official investigations; a defrocked cardinal and a convicted prelate; and then a scurrilous book revealing Vatican hypocrisy and sexual duplicity. We have endured a Lent of discontent and it makes us yearn for Easter's message of hope and new life more than ever before—survivors, victims, and their families, especially, and also all the lay women and men who were neither passively nor actively complicit in abuse or its cover-up but who have suffered so grievously. They are also innocent victims of the institutional dysfunction and the malignant clericalism that has seen the Church rightly lambasted for its sins of omission and commission.

During the Easter season, we need to walk and chew gum at the same time. While not trying to deny or spin the bad news stories that continue to shame us, we have to say, too, that we are an Easter people and Alleluia is our song. As the author of Ecclesiastes reminds us, there is a season and a time for everything. We are immersed in a dark night of the soul; yet we can glimpse the light of Christ piercing through the gloom.

I am always consoled at Easter by the hymns of Charles Wesley. Though I usually turn to his triumphant anthem "Christ the Lord Is Risen Today," this year, it is "Love Divine, All Loves Excelling" that has captured my imagination. Maybe I need to move away from any hint of triumphalism, albeit that it is God's triumph rather than the Church's that we celebrate on Easter Day and focus on the glory yet to come.

In any time or season, "Love Divine" is among the finest religious poetry and most theologically adroit hymns ever written. But this year, the third verse seems most apt:

Finish then thy new creation,
Pure and sinless let us be;
let us see thy great salvation,
perfectly restored in thee:
Changed from glory into glory,
Till in heav'n we take our place,
Till we cast our crowns before thee,
Lost in wonder, love and praise.

The phrase "Changed from glory into glory" is both a rendering of 2 Corinthians 3:18 and an echo of St. Irenaeus's famous line: "The glory of God is humanity fully alive." At our best, when we are living our Easter faith, we are already, imperfectly, reflections of God's glory. For this reason, this hymn is one of our great Easter hymns.

We are not defined by our worst sins. Most of us are doing our best to reflect God's glory. Through God raising Jesus from the dead, we are all invited to life eternal and to be caught up in the greatest outpouring of love ever known. As a result of Easter glory, we are meant to be the most loving people that we can possibly be.

The problem with the concept of love is that we have devalued the currency. We use the word too often of things we do not or cannot love. We say "I love you" to people we do not love, and because we've learned that actions are more telling than words, we don't easily believe others when they tell us they love us. We can feel unlovable and cynical about the whole experience.

However, we can be sure of three things. First, if we feel distant from God, we only need to guess who has moved away from whom; nothing we do stops God from loving us. Second, God loves us as we are, not as we would like to be. As the old saying goes, "You don't have to get good to get God, you have to get God to try and get good." Third, the song "You're Nobody till Somebody Loves You" reminds us that being vulnerable enough to tell those we love that we love them is no sentimental exercise but a participation in the heart of God. It is the taste on earth of the fullness of the Easter glory yet to come.

So, let's experience the power of God's absolute and unconditional love, so we may invite into our humble dwelling with the risen Christ, as Wesley wrote:

> Jesus, thou art all compassion,
> pure, unbounded love thou art.
> Visit us with thy salvation;
> enter ev'ry trembling heart.

We will need it for what lies ahead, but that is for another day.

50

OUR LADY OF THE ROSARY

Every time I say the Rosary, the seven-year-old boy in me comes out to pray because that was how old I was when I first went to "Oaklands"—Uncle Maurice's and Aunty Claire's property in outback Australia.

I come from a large extended Irish/Australian Catholic family. For twenty years, Maurice invited his thirty-two nieces and nephews to Oaklands for school holidays. There could be up to ten cousins there at a time.

Maurice and Claire married in 1948. Every night until Maurice died a few years ago, they said the Rosary. And even though the nightly devotion was falling off in our homes during the rebellious 1970s, when we went to Oaklands, we would all kneel and recite five decades after dinner. Because Maurice and Claire had become so used to each other's patterns of prayer, they had a very distinctive way of "giving out" the Hail Mary and responding with the Holy Mary. Maurice would say, *Hail Mare mingum, blest la jim.* By the time my uncle got to *mingum*, which I assume was "among women," Claire would start, *Whole may may mem*. And so, both phrases cascaded to become *Hail Mare mingum, blest la jim/ Whole may may mem*. They were talking in tongues long before it was trendy!

Eighteen years on from when I started holidaying on the family farm, I decided to enter the Jesuits. A week before I entered, my cousin, Paul Leonard, took me out for dinner. He spent more holidays at Oaklands then I did. Given what I was about to do with my life, matters religious were on the agenda. Out of nowhere and from across the table Paul said, *Hail Mare mingum, blest la jim* to which I immediately replied, *Whole may may mem*.

During the meal, we recalled memories of those holidays, until Paul said, "But there was that weird prayer Uncle Maurice used to say. Do you remember it? It's a bit strange don't you think to hit your chest and call out, 'Say g'day to Jesus,' and then reply, 'Have mercy on us.'" Now, this is an Australian moment, but my uncle had a very broad Australian accent. What my cousin thought was "Say g'day to Jesus" was, in fact, "Sacred Heart of Jesus." And, at that moment, I could hear my uncle saying it and could well understand how then seven-year-old Paul got it wrong and it stuck.

I now prefer Paul's masterful, inculturated version of the Litany to the Sacred Heart because, like Uncle Maurice's Rosary, it is filled with humanity and love.

There was something incongruous about those nightly devotions being enacted in such a harsh environment. There are few places to hide in the outback of Australia, and maybe that's why the affection for the Rosary took such root.

In concert with every other major religious tradition, the Rosary employs posture, beads, and mantras so that the repetition of it gets into our bones and the familial affections it evokes arrests our hearts. We don't need to think about it, we are just present and reassured.

Maurice and Claire gave us sane Mariology too, for at the end of the Rosary, Christ always got the last word. This is the way it should be. Always! These days, devotion to Mary is either dripping in piety or ignored altogether. Both extremes are to be avoided.

When I was ordained a priest, I received several volumes of a tome entitled *Mary Speaks to Her Priests*. After reading that book, I realized that it was filled with well-meaning but fundamental heresy. The Mother of the Lord is a full and true human being, but she is not God. If we believe she is in heaven, then she cannot be angry and upset with the world and her priests.

The Gospels tell a more confronting story: that she knew what it was to be an unmarried teenage mother, a refugee, a parent, who loses a child for days, misunderstands her son and is misunderstood by him, glories in his glory, watches him capitally punished, and is with his followers as they risk everything in going out in Christ's name. There are more than a few immediate and contemporary resonances in that list.

The Rosary is not a pious relic. In a hostile world, rote prayers are sometimes a buffer against harsh realities, and if they always lead us to Christ, then he sends us out to confront our world with humanity, mercy, and love.

51

"LORD, HELP MY UNBELIEF!"

As stated earlier, my first pastoral appointment was to St. Canice's parish, which included Kings Cross, the red-light district of Sydney. It was the steepest learning curve of my life, but I loved it, except for Halloween, All Souls' Day, and any Friday the 13th. Then every crazy person in town called in to share his or her experience of evil, the devil, and demonic possession.

On one occasion, my seventy-one-year-old parish priest, Father Donal Taylor, SJ, knocked on my door and said in his gentle Irish brogue, "There are two fellas in the parlor who need your particular gifts." And walked away.

As I entered the parlor, the men said, "Are you the expert? The old priest said he would get the expert for us."

I'd been set up!

Bradley and Gary had just moved into Kings Cross. Bradley was a handbag designer, and Gary designed women's shoes. They were the campiest men I had ever met.

"We've not been able to sleep since we moved into our unit because it's possessed. So, we want an expert like you to come and exorcise our home."

I would deal with Donal later!

I calmly explained that, while we sometimes exorcise people, these days we recommend psychiatry first, and we never exorcise places. I did, however, offer to do a house blessing, one of the most ancient and richest rituals we have. We arranged a date for four days hence.

"What do we need in preparation?" they asked.

I suggested they buy a cross or a religious icon, have a bowl of water ready to be blessed, and a candle for me to light during the ceremony. When I arrived at their unit, they had bought scores of crosses and icons now fashioned into a wave along the wall from their front door to the lounge room. It was spectacular! Then, I discovered twenty candles ablaze and on the table was a vat of water.

After I processed through the house sprinkling the now-holy water about, Bradley told me that I'd missed a room. "I don't think so," I said. "The loo, Father," he replied. (I wanted to suggest that if I blessed the cistern, he would be flushing holy water for days, but I refrained!)

As I was leaving, they handed me an envelope that I later learned contained two thousand dollars. When I handed it to Father Donal, he didn't miss a beat: "I knew they were quality guys. I hope you invited them to Sunday Mass."

Two weeks later, they were back in the parlor. I thought my house blessing had failed, but if they wanted their money back, I had not seen it since. But they had rushed to tell me that their next-door neighbor, Gwen, had arrived home that morning from a three-month overseas cruise and had come in to welcome them to the building. Gwen told them that their apartment hadn't sold for a year because of the double murder that occurred in their lounge room. This violent crime had never been disclosed to Gary and Bradley. All they knew was that something was not right in that place. The spirits were unsettled. Since my house blessing, however, they reported that they had slept like babies.

They both received an out-of-court settlement of sixty thousand dollars from the real estate agent. When I told Donal about these developments, he observed, "Well, I think it's only right that the blesser should get 10 percent of the blessings!"

They did better than that! A week later, they donated the entire sum to Caritas, the St. Vincent de Paul Society, and St. Canice's Soup Kitchen, and became regular parishioners.

I have always liked the accuracy of the baptismal question: "Do you reject evil in all its guises and all its empty promises?" I believe in external evil. When I think of the 36,000 people who will die today of malnutrition or the 60 million refugees in the world, or the dark thoughts I sometimes have, I know that evil exists.

What I struggle with is the personification of evil and the ease with which Pope Francis, following St. Ignatius of Loyola's lead, talks about the work of the devil, of Satan.

My hesitation is strange because it must be logically true that, if we can give ourselves to good and love—to God—then we must be able to surrender ourselves to hate and evil—to the devil. I know I'm suspicious of "the devil made me do it" theology, but the pope says that the devil's handiwork is seen in discouragement, hopeless-ness, cowardice, negativity, cynicism, and bitterness. I get that.

So maybe it's time for me to pray, "Lord, I believe, help my unbelief!"

52

GOD IS GOOD WITH MESS

During Advent one year, a religious sister invited me to be the guest of honor at her primary school's nativity play. There were twenty-five eight-year-old children who were to be in this year's cast.

When I arrived, sister told me that she had trouble with the boy who was playing the innkeeper because he wanted to play St. Joseph. "Ahmed is a Muslim boy, and I really thought I should have a Christian boy playing St. Joseph." Rehearsals had not gone well, but she was sure that the performance would be fine.

The whole school gathered along with the parents of the children in year three. In the front row of the school hall was the principal, sister, and me.

Everything about the play went along as expected until the moment when Mary and Joseph arrived at the inn. Joseph knocked on the makeshift door. The innkeeper, whom we could clearly see, yelled out gruffly, "Who's there?"

"I am Joseph, and this is my wife, Mary. We have nowhere to stay tonight, and she's having a baby." (Having a baby? If her baby bump was anything to go by, that girl was having octuplets!)

The innkeeper didn't budge. Sister lent forward in a loud stage whisper and said, "Ahmed, you know what to do, darling. Open the door and make your wonderful speech." He didn't move.

So, sister told Joseph to knock again. The innkeeper barked more angrily, "Who's there?" We got Joseph's speech again, but the little innkeeper wasn't having any of it.

The tension was rising in the hall now, so sister lent forward again and in a stronger voice said, "Ahmed, your mom and dad are here, darling, and they'll be so proud of you." He was impassive.

Sister then told Joseph to knock for the third time, and he gave out his speech yet again. Before Ahmed could decide what to do next, a loud African bass voice came from the back of the room, "Ahmed, you open that God-damn door, or I'll belt your bum!" I turned around to see the largest human being I have ever seen.

Ahmed's father, Mohammed, was a refugee to Australia from Sierra Leone. He was six feet, eight inches tall and later told me that he was a solid seventeen stone (238 lbs.). He was so proud that his son had a starring role in the Christmas play that he wore his magnificent white celebratory kaftan with a white cap on his head. Now, however, he was coming down the aisle toward the stage, and every adult present was thinking, "Open the door, open the door, open that God-damn door, because I think that being belted by this guy is going to hurt."

DISCIPLESHIP

Someone intercepted Mohammed as Ahmed opened the door and said plaintively to Mary, "You can come in," but then shouted at Joseph, "but Joseph, you can piss off!" With that, Joseph burst into tears, the shepherds and angels started to hit the innkeeper "because he said a rude word," and the children in the audience chanted, "Fight! Fight! Fight!"

Sister stood up, turned to everyone, and said, "This isn't the way I rehearsed it." It took ten minutes for her to reclaim some peace on earth.

It was the best nativity play I have ever seen because God is good with mess.

⚜✝⚜

The first Christmas must have been a very messy affair. I know there is a long tradition that holds that Jesus's birth was as miraculous as his conception, but if his birth was not like yours and mine, then our doctrine of Jesus's full and true humanity is severely challenged.

I find it even more moving to reflect on the experience of a thirteen-year-old girl and her nineteen-year-old husband traveling about a hundred miles (160 kilometers) from Nazareth to Bethlehem in the final weeks of her pregnancy. On arrival, they find themselves homeless, and at least in one tradition, Jesus is born in a cave or stable where the animals were housed. Imagine the smell. This is far from the sanitized image that we have on our Christmas cards or of which we sing in our carols.

No one predicted the way God would send us a Savior. No one envisaged that the first witnesses to his birth would be illiterate, non-temple-going shepherds.

And, while some waited for a mercenary to overthrow the Romans, and others held their breath for the procession of a great and grand king, heaven and earth became one in a poor, defenseless, messy baby, who shows us the way out of our own mess, who is our truth, and who leads us to the fullness of life in this world and the next.